CONTENTS

Preface

Rhetoric and Eloquence

The Exordium or Introduction

The Narration

Division and Argument

The Peroration

Passion and Persuasion

The Study of Words

Elegance and Grace

Composition and Style

Copiousness of Words

Knowledge and Self-confidence

Conclusion

PREFACE

The power of eloquence to move and persuade men is universally recognized. To-day the public speaker plays a vital part in the solution of every great question and problem. Oratory, in the true sense, is not a lost art, but a potent means of imparting information, instruction, and persuasion.

Eloquence is still "the appropriate organ of the highest personal energy." As one has well said, "The orator is not compelled to wait through long and weary years to reap the reward of his labors. His triumphs are instantaneous."

And again, "To stand up before a vast assembly composed of men of the most various callings, views, passions, and prejudices, and mold them at will; to play upon their hearts and minds as a master upon the keys of a piano; to convince their understandings by the logic, and to thrill their feelings by the art of the orator; to see every eye watching his face, and every ear intent on the words that drop from his lips; to see indifference changed to breathless interest, and aversion to rapturous enthusiasm; to hear thunders of applause at the close of every period; to see the whole assembly animated by the feelings which in him are burning and struggling for utterance; and to think that all this is the creation of the moment, and has sprung instantaneously from his fiery brain and the inspiration imparted to it by the circumstances of the hour;—*this*, perhaps, is the greatest triumph of which the human mind is capable, and that in which its divinity is most signally revealed."

The aims and purposes of speaking to-day have radically changed from former times. Deliberative bodies, composed of busy men, meet now to discuss and dispose of grave and weighty business. There is little necessity nor scope for eloquence. Time is too valuable to permit of prolonged speaking. Men are tacitly expected to "get to the point," and to be reasonably brief in what they have to say.

Under these circumstances certain extravagant types of old-time oratory would be ineffectual to-day. The stentorian and dramatic tones, with hand inserted in the breast of the coat, with exaggerated facial expression, and studied posture, would make a speaker to-day an object of ridicule.

This applies equally to speech in the law court, pulpit, on the lecture platform, and in other departments of public address. The implicit demand everywhere is that the speaker should say what he has to say naturally, simply, and concisely.

This does not mean, however, that he must confine himself to plain statement of fact, with no manifestation of feeling or earnestness. Men are still influenced and persuaded by impassioned speech. There is nothing incompatible between deep feeling and clear-cut speech. A man having profound convictions upon any subject of importance will always speak on it with fervor and sincerity.

The widespread interest in the subject of public speaking has suggested this adaptation of Quintilian's celebrated work on the education of the orator. This work has long been regarded as one of the most valuable treatises ever written on oratory, but in its original form it is ponderous and inaccessible to the average reader. In the present abridged and modernized form it may be read and studied with benefit by earnest students of the art of public speaking.

A brief account of Quintilian says: "Quintilianus, M. Fabius, was born at Calagurris, in Spain, A. D. 40. He completed his education at Rome, and began to practise at the bar about 68. But he was chiefly distinguished as a teacher of eloquence, bearing away the palm in his department from all his rivals, and associating his name, even to a proverb, with preeminence in the art. By Domitian he was invested with the insignia and title of consul, and is, moreover, celebrated as the first public instructor who, in virtue of the endowment by Vespasian, received a regular salary from the imperial exchequer. He is supposed to have died about 118. The great work of Quintilian is a complete system of rhetoric, in twelve books, entitled *De Institutione Oratoria Libre XII,* or sometimes *Institutiones Oratoriæ,* dedicated to his friend Marcellus Victorius, himself a celebrated orator, and a favorite at Court. This production bears throughout the impress of a clear, sound judgment, keen discrimination, and pure taste, improved by extensive reading, deep reflection, and long practise."

The text used for this condensation is from the version of J. Patsall, A.M., London, 1774, according to the Paris edition by Professor Rollin. Many parts of the original work have been re-written or abridged, while several chapters have been entirely omitted.

GRENVILLE KLEISER

New York City,
August, 1919.

RHETORIC AND ELOQUENCE

WHAT RHETORIC IS

Rhetoric has been commonly defined as "The power of persuading." This opinion originated with Isocrates, if the work ascribed to him be really his; not that he intended to dishonor his profession, tho he gives us a generous idea of rhetoric by calling it the workmanship of persuasion. We find almost the same thing in the Gorgias of Plato, but this is the opinion of that rhetorician, and not of Plato. Cicero has written in many places that the duty of an orator is to speak in "a manner proper to persuade"; and in his books of rhetoric, of which undoubtedly he does not approve himself, he makes the end of eloquence to consist in persuasion.

But does not money likewise persuade? Is not credit, the authority of the speaker, the dignity of a respectable person, attended with the same effect? Even without speaking a word, the remembrance of past services, the appearance of distress, a beautiful aspect, make deep impressions on minds and are decisive in their favor.

Did Antonius, pleading the cause of M. Aquilius, trust to the force of his reasons when he abruptly tore open his garment and exposed to view the honorable wounds he received fighting for his country? This act of his forced streams of tears from the eyes of the Roman people, who, not able to resist so moving a spectacle, acquitted the criminal. Sergius Galba escaped the severity of the laws by appearing in court with his own little children, and the son of Gallus Sulpitius, in his arms. The sight of so many wretched objects melted the judges into compassion. This we find equally attested by some of our historians and by a speech of Cato. What shall I say of the example of Phryne, whose beauty was of more service in her cause than all the eloquence of Hyperides; for tho his pleading was admirable in her defense, yet perceiving it to be without effect, by suddenly laying open her tunic he disclosed the naked beauty of her bosom, and made the judges sensible that she had as many charms for them as for others. Now, if all these instances persuade, persuasion, then, can not be the end of rhetoric.

Some, therefore, have seemed to themselves rather more exact who, in the main of the same way of thinking, define rhetoric as the "Power of persuading by speaking." It is to this that Gorgias, in the book above cited, is at last reduced by Socrates. Theodectes does not much differ from them, if the work ascribed to him be his, or Aristotle's. In this book the end of rhetoric is supposed to be "The leading of men wherever one pleases by the faculty of speaking." But this definition is not sufficiently comprehensive. Many others besides the orator persuade by their words and lead minds in whatever direction they please.

Some, therefore, as Aristotle, setting aside the consideration of the end, have defined rhetoric to be "The power of inventing whatever is persuasive in a discourse." This definition is equally as faulty as that just mentioned, and is likewise defective in another respect, as including only invention, which, separate from elocution, can not constitute a speech.

It appears from Plato's Gorgias that he was far from regarding rhetoric as an art of ill tendency, but that, rather it is, or ought to be, if we were to conceive an adequate idea of it inseparable from virtue. This he explains more clearly in his Phædrus, where he says that "The art can never be perfect without an exact knowledge and strict observance of justice." I join him in this opinion, and if these were not his real sentiments, would he have written an apology for Socrates and the eulogium of those brave citizens who lost their lives in the defense of their country? This is certainly acting the part of an orator, and if in any respect he attacks the profession, it is on account of those who make ill use of eloquence. Socrates, animated with the same spirit, thought it unworthy of him to pronounce the speech Lysias had composed for his defense, it being the custom of the orators of those times to write speeches for arraigned criminals, which the latter pronounced in their own defense; thus eluding the law that prohibited pleading for another. Plato, likewise, in his Phædrus, condemns the masters that separated rhetoric from justice, and preferred probabilities to truth.

Such are the definitions of rhetoric which have been principally set forth. To go through all of them is not my purpose, nor do I think it possible, as most writers on arts have shown a perverse dislike for defining things as others do or in the same terms as those who wrote before them. I am far from being influenced by a like spirit of ambition, and far from flattering myself with the glory of invention, and I shall rest content with that which seems most rational, that rhetoric is properly defined as "The science of speaking well." Having found what is best, it is useless to seek further.

Accepting this definition, therefore, it will be no difficult matter to ascertain its end, for if it be "The science of speaking well," then "to speak well" will be the end it proposes to itself.

THE USE OF RHETORIC

The next question is on the utility of rhetoric, and from this point of view some direct the bitterest invectives against it, and what is very unbecoming, exert the force of eloquence against eloquence, saying that by it the wicked are freed from punishment, and the innocent opprest by its artifices; that it perverts good counsel, and enforces bad; that it foments troubles and seditions in States; that it arms nations against each other, and makes them irreconcilable enemies; and that its power is never more manifest than when error and lies triumph over truth.

Comic poets reproach Socrates with teaching how to make a bad cause good, and Plato represents Lysias and Gorgias boasting the same thing. To these may be added several examples of Greeks and Romans, and a long list of orators whose eloquence was not only the ruin of private persons, but even destructive to whole cities and republics; and for this reason it was that eloquence was banished from Sparta and so restricted at Athens that the orator was not allowed to make appeal to the passions.

Granting all this as sound argument, we must draw this necessary inference, that neither generals of armies, nor magistrates, nor medicine, nor philosophy, will be of any use. Flaminius, an imprudent general, lost one of our armies. The Gracchi Saturninus, and Glaucia, to raise themselves to dignity, put Rome into an uproar. Physicians often administer poisons, and among philosophers some have been found guilty of the most enormous crimes. Let us not eat of the meats with which our tables are spread, for meats frequently have caused disease. Let us never go into houses; they may fall and crush us to death. Let not our soldiers be armed with swords; a robber may use the same weapon against us. In short, who does not know that the most necessary things in life, as air, fire, water, nay, even the celestial bodies, are sometimes very injurious to our well-being?

But how many examples can be quoted in our favor? Did not Appius the Blind, by the force of his eloquence dissuade the Senate from making a shameful peace with Pyrrhus? Did not Cicero's divine eloquence appear more popular than the Agrarian law he attacked? Did it not disconcert the audacious measures of Cataline? And did not he, even in his civil capacity, obtain by it honors that are conferred on only the most illustrious conquerors? Is it not the orator who strengthens the soldier's drooping courage, who animates him amidst the greatest dangers, and inspires him to choose a glorious death rather than a life of infamy?

The example of the Romans, among whom eloquence always has been held in the greatest veneration, shall have a higher place in my regard than that of the Spartans and Athenians. It is not to be supposed that the founders of cities could have made a united people of a vagabond multitude without the charms of persuasive words, nor that law-givers, without extraordinary talent for speaking, could have forced men to bend their necks to the yoke of the laws. Even the precepts of moral life, tho engraved on our hearts by the finger of nature, are more efficacious to inspire our hearts with love for them when their beauty is displayed by the ornaments of eloquent speech. Tho the arms of eloquence may harm and benefit equally, we must not, therefore, look on that as bad which may be put to a good use. Doubts of this kind may well be entertained by such as make "the force persuasion the end of eloquence," but we who constitute it "The science of speaking well," resolved to acknowledge none but the good man an orator, must naturally judge that its advantage is very considerable.

Certainly, the gracious Author of all beings and Maker of the world, has distinguished us from the animals in no respect more than by the gift of speech. They surpass us in bulk, in strength, in the supporting of toil, in speed, and stand less in need of outside help. Guided by nature only, they learn sooner to walk, to seek for their food, and to swim over rivers. They have on their bodies sufficient covering to guard them against cold; all of them have their natural weapons of defense; their food lies, in a manner, on all sides of them; and we, indigent beings! to what anxieties are we put in securing these things? But God, a beneficent parent, gave us reason for our portion, a gift which makes us partakers of a life of immortality. But this reason would be of little use to us, and we would be greatly perplexed to make it known, unless we could express by words our thoughts. This is what animals lack, more than thought and understanding, of which it can not be said they are entirely destitute. For to make themselves secure and commodious lodges, to interweave their nests with such art, to rear their young with such care, to teach them to shift for themselves when grown up, to hoard provisions for the winter, to produce such inimitable works as wax and honey, are instances perhaps of a glimmering of reason; but because destitute of speech, all the extraordinary things they do can not distinguish them from the brute part of creation. Let us consider dumb persons: how does the heavenly soul, which takes form in their bodies, operate in them? We perceive, indeed, that its help is but weak, and its action but languid.

THE VALUE OF THE GIFT OF SPEECH

If, then, the beneficent Creator of the world has not imparted to us a greater blessing than the gift of speech, what can we esteem more deserving of our labor and improvement, and what object is more worthy of our ambition than that of raising ourselves above other men by the same means by which they raise themselves above beasts, so much the more as no labor is attended with a more abundant harvest of glory? To be convinced of this we need only consider by what degrees eloquence has been brought to the perfection in which we now see it, and how far it might still be perfected. For, not to mention the advantage and pleasure a good man reaps from defending his friends, governing the Senate by his counsels, seeing himself the oracle of the people, and master of armies, what can be more noble than by the faculty of speaking and thinking, which is common to all men, to erect for himself such a standard of praise and glory as to seem to the minds of men not so much to discourse and speak, but, like Pericles, to make his words thunder and lightning.

THE ART OF SPEAKING

There would be no end were I to expatiate to the limit of my inclination on the subject of the gift of speech and its utility. I shall pass, therefore, to the following question, "Whether rhetoric be an art?" Those who wrote rules for eloquence doubted so little its being so, that they prefixt no other title to their books than "The art of speaking." Cicero says that what we call rhetoric is only an artificial eloquence. If this were an opinion peculiar to orators, it might be thought that they intended it as a mark of dignity attached to their studies, but most philosophers, stoics as well as peripatetics, concur in this opinion. I must confess I had some doubt about discussing this matter, lest I might seem diffident of its truth; for who can be so devoid of sense and knowledge as to find art in architecture, in weaving, in pottery, and imagine that rhetoric, the excellence of which we have already shown, could arrive at its present state of grandeur and perfection without the direction of art? I am persuaded that those of the contrary opinion were so more for the sake of exercising their wit on the singularity of the subject than from any real conviction.

IS ELOQUENCE A GIFT OF NATURE?

Some maintain that rhetoric is a gift of nature, yet admit that it may be helped by exercise. Antonius, in Cicero's books of the Orator, calls it a sort of observation and not an art. But this opinion is not there asserted as truth, but only to keep up the character of Antonius, who was a connoisseur at concealing art. Lysias seems to be of the same opinion, which he defends by saying that the most simple and ignorant people possess a kind of rhetoric when they speak for themselves. They find something like an exordium, they make a narration, they prove, refute, and their prayers and entreaties have the force of a peroration. Lysias and his adherents proceed afterward to vain subtleties. "That which is the effect of art," say they, "could not have existed before art. In all times men have known how to speak for themselves and against others, but masters of rhetoric have been only of a late date, first known about the time of Tisias and Corax; therefore oratorical speech was prior to art, consequently it could not be the result of art, and therefore, rhetoric is not an art." We shall not endeavor to enquire into the time when rhetoric began to be taught, but this we may say, that it is certain Homer makes mention not only of Phœnix, who was a master, skilled in both speaking and fighting, but also of many other orators. We may observe likewise from Homer, that all the parts of a discourse are found in the speech of the three captains deputed to Achilles, that several young men dispute for the prize of eloquence, and that among other ornaments of sculpture on the buckler of Achilles, Vulcan did not forget law-causes and the pleaders of them.

It will be sufficient, however, to answer that "Everything perfected by art has its source in nature." If it were not so, we should exclude medicine from the catalog of arts, the discovery of which was owing to observations made on things conducive or harmful to public health, and in the opinion of some it is wholly grounded on experiments. Before it was reduced to an art, tents and bandages were applied to wounds, rest and abstinence cured fever; not that the reason of all this was then known, but the nature of the ailment indicated such curative methods and forced men to this regimen. In like manner architecture can not be an art, the first men having built their cottages without its direction. Music must undergo the same charge, as every nation has its own peculiarities in dancing and singing. Now, if by rhetoric be meant any kind of speech, I must own it prior to art; but if not everyone who speaks is an orator, and if in the primitive ages of the world men did not speak orator-like, the orator, consequently, must have been made so by art, and therefore could not exist before it.

RHETORIC AND MISREPRESENTATION

The next objection is not one so much in reality as it is a mere cavil; that "Art never assents to false opinions, because it can not be constituted as such without precepts, which are always true; but rhetoric assents to what is false, therefore it is not an art." I admit that sometimes rhetoric says false things instead of true, but it does not follow that it assents to what is false. There is a wide difference between assenting to a falsehood, and making others assent to it. So it is that a general of an army often has recourse to stratagems. When Hannibal perceived himself to be blocked up by Fabius, he ordered faggots of brush-wood to be fastened about the horns of some oxen, and fire being set to the faggots, had the cattle driven up the mountains in the night, in order to make the enemy believe he was about to decamp. But this was only a false alarm, for he himself very well knew what his scheme was. When Theopompus the Spartan, by changing clothes with his wife, made his escape out of prison, the deception was not imposed upon himself, but upon his guards. Thus, when an orator speaks falsehood instead of truth, he knows what he is about; he does not yield to it himself, his intention being to deceive others. When Cicero boasted that he threw darkness on the minds of the judges, in the cause of Cluentius, could it be said that he himself was unacquainted with all the intricacies of his method of confusing their understanding of the facts? Or shall a painter who so disposes his objects that some seem to project from the canvas, others to sink in, be supposed not to know that they are all drawn on a plain surface?

THE OBJECT OF A SPEECH

It is again objected that "Every art proposes to itself an end; but rhetoric has no end, or does not put into execution the end it proposes to itself." This is false, as is shown from what already has been said concerning the end of rhetoric and in what it consists. The orator will never fail to obtain this end, for he always will speak well. This objection, therefore, can affect only those who make persuasion the end of rhetoric; but our orator, and our definition of art, are not restricted to events. An orator, indeed, strives to gain his cause; but suppose he loses it, as long as he has pleaded well he fulfils the injunctions of his art. A pilot desires to come safe into port, but if a storm sweeps away his ship, is he, on that account, a less experienced pilot? His keeping constantly to the helm is sufficient proof that he was not neglecting his duty. A physician tries to cure a sick person, but if his remedies are hindered in their operation by either the violence of the disease, the intemperance of the patient, or some unforeseen accident, he is not to be blamed, because he has satisfied all the directions of his art. So it is with the orator, whose end is to speak well; for it is in the act, and not in the effect, that art consists, as I shall soon make clear. Therefore, it is false to say that "Art knows when it has obtained its end, but rhetoric knows nothing of the matter," as if an orator could be ignorant of his speaking well and to the purpose.

But it is said, further, that rhetoric, contrary to the custom of all other arts, adopts vice, because it countenances falsehood and moves the passions. Neither of these are bad practises, and consequently not vicious, when grounded on substantial reasons. To disguise truth is sometimes allowable even in the sage, and if a judge can not be brought to do justice except by means of the passions, the orator must necessarily have recourse to them. Very often the judges appointed to decide are ignorant, and there is necessity for changing their wrongly conceived opinions, to keep them from error. Should there be a bench, a tribunal, an assembly of wise and learned judges whose hearts are inaccessible to hatred, envy, hope, fear, prejudice, and the impositions of false witnesses, there would be little occasion for the exertions of eloquence and all that might seem requisite would be only to amuse the ear with the harmony of cadence. But if the orator has to deal with light, inconstant, prejudiced, and corrupt judges, and if many embarrassments must be removed in order to throw light upon truth, then artful stratagem must fight the battle, and set all its engines to work, for he who is beaten out of the straight road can not get into it again except by another turnabout.

ELOQUENCE ACQUIRED BY STUDY AND PRACTISE

These are the principal objections which have been made against rhetoric. There are others of less moment but derived from the same source. That rhetoric is an art is thus briefly demonstrated. If art, as Cleanthes thinks, is a power which prepares a way and establishes an order, can it be doubted that we must keep to a certain way and a certain order for speaking well? And if, according to the most generally accepted opinion, we ought to call art, everything which by a combination of agreeing and co-exercised principles conducts to a useful end, have we not already shown that nothing of all this is lacking in rhetoric? Has it not, likewise, the two constituent parts of other arts, theory and practise? Again, if dialect be an art, as it is granted, for the same reason; so is rhetoric an art, the chief difference lying not so much in the genus as in the species. But we must not forget this observation, that art must be where a thing is done according to rule, and not at random; and art must be where he who has learned succeeds better than he who has not learned. But in matter of eloquence not only will the ignorant person be surpassed by the learned, but also the learned by the more learned; otherwise we should not have so many rules nor so many excellent masters. This ought to be acknowledged by all, but more especially by us who do not separate eloquence from the man of integrity.

THE EXORDIUM OR INTRODUCTION

The exordium, or introduction, is that part of the discourse which is pronounced before the subject is entered upon. As musicians make a prelude for obtaining silence and attention before they play their selections, so orators, before they begin their cause, have specified by the same application that which they say by way of preface for securing for themselves a kindly feeling in the listeners.

THE PURPOSE OF THE INTRODUCTION

The reason for an exordium is to dispose the auditors to be favorable to us in the other parts of the discourse. This, as most authors agree, is accomplished by making them friendly, attentive, and receptive, tho due regard should be paid to these three particulars throughout the whole of a speech.

Sometimes the exordium is applicable to the pleader of the cause, who, tho he ought to speak very little of himself, and always modestly, will find it of vast consequence to create a good opinion of himself and to make himself thought to be an honest man. So it is he will be regarded not so much as a zealous advocate, as a faithful and irreproachable witness. His motives for pleading must, therefore, appear to proceed not from tie of kindred, or friendship, but principally from a desire to promote the public good, if such motive can be urged, or any other important consideration. This conduct will befit plaintiffs in a much greater degree, that they may seem to have brought their action for just and weighty reasons, or were even compelled to do it from necessity.

As nothing else gives so great a sanction to the authority of the speaker as to be free from all suspicion of avarice, hatred, and ambition, so, also, there is a sort of tacit recommendation of ourselves if we profess our weak state and inability for contending with the superior genius and talents of the advocate of the other side. We are naturally disposed to favor the weak and opprest, and a conscientious judge hears an orator willingly whom he presumes not to be capable of making him swerve from his fixt purpose of doing justice. Hence the care of the ancients for concealing their talents.

IDEAS TO AVOID AND TO INCLUDE

All contemptuous, spiteful, haughty, calumniating expressions must be avoided and not so much as even insinuated to the defamation of any particular person or rank, much less against those to whom an affront would alienate the minds of the judges. To be so imprudent as to attack judges themselves, not openly, but in any indirect manner, would be most unwise.

The advocate for the other side may likewise furnish sufficient matter for an exordium. Sometimes honorable mention may be made of him, as when we pretend to be in dread of his interest and eloquence in order to make them suspected by the judges, and sometimes by casting odium on him, altho this must be done very seldom. I rather think, from the authority of the best authors, that whatever affects the orator, affects also the cause he patronizes, as it is natural for a judge to give more credit to those whom he more willingly hears.

We shall procure the favor of the judge not so much by praising him, which ought to be done with moderation, and is common to both sides, but rather by making his praise fitting, and connecting it with the interest of our cause. Thus, in speaking for a person of consequence, we may lay some stress on the judge's own dignity; for one of mean condition, on his justice; for the unhappy, on his mercy; for the injured, on his severity.

STUDYING YOUR HEARERS

It also would not be amiss to become acquainted, if possible, with his character. For, according as his temper is, harsh or mild, pleasant or grave, severe or easy, the cause should be made to incline toward the side which corresponds with his disposition, or to admit some mitigation or softening where it runs counter to it.

It may happen sometimes, too, that the judge is our enemy, or the opponent's friend. This is a circumstance requiring the circumspection of both parties, yet I think the favored advocate should behave with great caution, for a judge of a biased disposition will sometimes choose to pass sentence against his friends, or in favor of those to whom he bears enmity, that he may not appear to act with injustice.

AROUSING EMOTIONS

Judges have also their private opinions and prejudices, which we must either strengthen or weaken, according as we see necessary. Fear, too, sometimes must be removed, as Cicero, in his defense of Milo, endeavors to assure the judges that Pompey's army, drawn up about the Forum, is for their protection; and sometimes there will be an occasion to intimidate them, as the same orator does in one of his pleadings against Verres.

There are two ways of proceeding in this last case, the first plausible, and frequently used, as when it is hinted to them that the Roman people might entertain an ill opinion of them, or that there might be an appeal from their judgment; the other desperate, and not so much used, as when threatened with prosecution themselves if they suffer themselves to be corrupted. This is a hazardous point, and is conducted with more safety to the orator when in a large assembly where corrupt judges are restrained by fear, and the upright have the majority. But I would never counsel this before a single judge, unless every other resource was wanting. If necessity requires it, I can not say that it is the business of the art of oratory to give directions in the matter, any more than to lodge an appeal, tho that, too, is often of service, or to cite the judge in justice before he passes sentence, for to threaten, denounce, or indict may be done by any one else as well as the orator.

If the cause itself should furnish sufficient reason for gaining the good will of the judge, out of this whatever is most specious and favorable may be inserted in the exordium. It will be unnecessary to enumerate all the favorable circumstances in causes, they being easily known from the state of facts; besides, no exact enumeration can take place on account of the great diversity of law-suits. It is the cause itself, therefore, that must teach us to find and improve these circumstances; and, in like manner, with a circumstance that may make against us the cause will inform us how it may either be made entirely void, or at least invalidated.

From the cause compassion also sometimes arises, whether we have already suffered or are likely to suffer anything grievous. For I am not of the opinion of those who to distinguish the exordium from the peroration, will have the one to speak of what is past and the other of what is to come. They are sufficiently distinguished without this discrimination. In the exordium the orator ought to be more reserved, and ought only to throw out some hints of the sentiments of compassion he designs to excite in the minds of the judges; whereas in the peroration he may pour out all the passions, introduce persons speaking, and make the dead to come forth, as it were, out of their graves, and recommend to the judges the care of their dearest pledges. All these particulars are seldom executed in the exordium. But the manner just pointed out, it will be very proper to observe in it, and to wear down all impressions to the contrary made by the opposite side, that as our situation will be deplorable if we should be defeated in our expectations, so, on the other hand, the behavior of our opponent would be insolent and haughty.

MATERIAL FOR THE INTRODUCTION

Besides persons and causes, the exordium likewise is sometimes taken from their adjuncts, that is, from things relating to the cause and persons. To persons are applicable not only the pledges above mentioned, but affinities, friendships, sometimes cities and whole countries are also likely to suffer by the person's misfortunes.

Theophrastus adds another kind of exordium, taken from the pleading of the orator who speaks first. Such seems to be that of Demosthenes for Ctesiphon, in which he requests the judges to please permit him to reply as he thinks suitable rather than to follow the rules prescribed by the accuser.

As the confidence observable in some orators may easily pass for arrogance, there are certain ways of behavior which, tho common, will please, and therefore ought not to be neglected, to prevent their being used by the opposing side: these are wishing, warding off suspicion, supplicating, and making a show of trouble and anxiety.

The judge's attention is secured by inducing him to believe that the matter under debate is new, important, extraordinary, or of a heinous nature, or that it equally interests him and the public. Then his mind is to be roused and agitated by hope, fear, remonstrance, entreaty, and even by flattery, if it is thought that will be of any use. Another way of procuring attention may be to promise that we shall take up but little of their time, as we shall confine ourselves to the subject.

From what has been said, it appears that different causes require to be governed by different rules; and five kinds of causes are generally specified, which are said to be, either honest, base, doubtful, extraordinary, or obscure. Some add shameful, as a sixth kind, which others include in base or extraordinary. By extraordinary is understood that which is contrary to the opinion of men. In a doubtful cause the judge should be made favorable; in an obscure, docile; in a base, attentive. An honest cause is sufficient of itself to procure favor. Extraordinary and base causes lack remedies.

TWO TYPES OF INTRODUCTIONS

Some, therefore, specify two kinds of exordiums, one a beginning, the other an insinuation. In the first the judges are requested openly to give their good will and attention; but as this can not take place in the base kind of cause, the insinuation must steal in upon their minds, especially when the cause does not seem to appear with a sufficiently honest aspect, either because the thing itself is wicked, or is a measure not approved by the public. There are many instances of causes of unseemly appearance, as when general odium is incurred by opposing a patriot; and a like hostility ensues from acting against a father, a wretched old man, the blind, or the orphan.

This may be a general rule for the purpose, "To touch but slightly on the things that work against us, and to insist chiefly on those which are for our advantage." If the cause can not be so well maintained, let us have recourse to the goodness of the person, and if the person is not condemnable, let us ground our support on the cause. If nothing occurs to help us out, let us see what may hurt the opponent. For, since to obtain more favor is a thing to be wished, so the next step to it is to incur less hatred.

In things that can not be denied, we must endeavor to show that they are greatly short of what they are reported to be, or that they have been done with a different intention, or that they do not in any wise belong to the present question, or that repentance will make sufficient amends for them, or that they have already received a proportionate punishment. Herein, therefore, it will be better and more suitable for an advocate to act than for the person himself; because when pleading for another he can praise without the imputation of arrogance, and sometimes can even reprove with advantage.

Insinuation seems to be not less necessary when the opponent's action has pre-possest the minds of the judges, or when they have been fatigued by the tediousness of the pleading. The first may be got the better of by promising substantial proofs on our side, and by refuting those of the opponent. The second, by giving hopes of being brief, and by having recourse to the means prescribed for making the judge attentive. In the latter case, too, some seasonable pleasantry, or anything witty to freshen the mind will have a good effect. It will not be amiss, likewise, to remove any seeming obstruction. As Cicero says of himself, he is not unaware that some will find it strange that he, who for so many years had defended such a number of people, and had given no offense to anyone, should undertake to accuse Verres. Afterward he shows that if, on the one hand, he accuses Verres, still, on the other, he defends the allies of the Roman people.

HOW TO SELECT THE RIGHT BEGINNING

The orator should consider what the subject is upon which he is to speak, before whom, for whom, against whom, at what time, in what place, under what conditions, what the public think of it, what the judges may think of it before they hear him, and what he himself has to desire, and what to apprehend. Whoever makes these reflections will know where he should naturally begin. But now orators call exordium anything with which they begin, and consider it of advantage to make the beginning with some brilliant thought. Undoubtedly many things are taken into the exordium which are drawn from other parts of the cause or at least are common to them, but nothing in either respect is better said than that which can not be said so well elsewhere.

THE VALUE OF NATURALNESS

There are many very engaging things in an exordium which is framed from the opponent's pleading, and this is because it does not seem to favor of the closet, but is produced on the spot and comes from the very thing. By its easy, natural turn, it enhances the reputation of genius. Its air of simplicity, the judge not being on his guard against it, begets belief, and tho the discourse in all other parts be elaborate and written with great accuracy, it will for the most part seem an extempore oration, the exordium evidently appearing to have nothing premeditated.

But nothing else will so well suit an exordium as modesty in the countenance, voice, thoughts, and composition, so that even in an uncontrovertible kind of cause, too great confidence ought not to display itself. Security is always odious in a pleader, and a judge who is sensible of his authority tacitly demands respect.

An orator must likewise be exceedingly careful to keep himself from being suspected, particularly in that regard; therefore, not the least show of study should be made, because all his art will seem exerted against the judge, and not to show this is the greatest perfection of art. This rule has been recommended by all authors, and undoubtedly with good reason, but sometimes is altered by circumstances, because in certain causes the judges themselves require studied discourses, and fancy themselves thought mean of unless accuracy appears in thought and expression. It is of no significance to instruct them; they must be pleased. It is indeed difficult to find a medium in this respect, but the orator may so temper his manner as to speak with justness, and not with too great a show of art.

THE NEED OF SIMPLICITY OF EXPRESSION

Another rule inculcated by the ancients is not to admit into the exordium any strange word, too bold a metaphor, an obsolete expression, or a poetical turn. As yet we are not favorably received by the auditors, their attention is not entirely held, but when once they conceive an esteem and are warmly inclined toward us, then is the time to hazard this liberty, especially when we enter upon parts the natural fertility of which does not allow the liberty of expression to be noticed amidst the luster spread about it.

The style of the exordium ought not to be like that of the argument proper and the narration, neither ought it to be finely spun out, or harmonized into periodical cadences, but, rather, it should be simple and natural, promising neither too much by words nor countenance. A modest action, also, devoid of the least suspicion of ostentation, will better insinuate itself into the mind of the auditor. But these ought to be regulated according to the sentiments we would have the judges imbibe from us.

It must be remembered, however, that nowhere is less allowance made than here for failing in memory or appearing destitute of the power of articulating many words together. An ill-pronounced exordium may well be compared to a visage full of scars, and certainly he must be a bad pilot who puts his ship in danger of sinking, as he is going out of port.

In regard to the length of the exordium, it ought to be proportionate to the nature of the cause. Simple causes admit of a shorter exordium; the complex, doubtful, and odious, require a longer exordium. Some writers have prescribed four points as laws for all exordiums,—which is ridiculous. An immoderate length should be equally avoided, lest it appear, as some monsters, bigger in the head than in the rest of the body, and create disgust where it ought only to prepare.

"TYING UP" THE INTRODUCTION

As often as we use an exordium, whether we pass next to the narration, or immediately to the proofs, we ought always to preserve a connection between what follows and what goes before. To proceed from one part to another, by some ingenious thought which disguises the transition, and to seek applause from such a studied exertion of wit, is quite of a piece with the cold and childish affectation of our declaimers. If a long and intricate narration must follow, the judge ought naturally to be prepared for it. This Cicero often does, as in this passage: "I must proceed pretty high to clear up this matter to you, which I hope, gentlemen, you will not be displeased at, because its origin being known will make you thoroughly acquainted with the particulars proceeding from it."

THE NARRATION

There are causes so short as to require rather to be proposed than told. It is sometimes the case with two contending sides, either that they have no exposition to make, or that agreeing on the fact, they contest only the right. Sometimes one of the contending parties, most commonly the plaintiff, need only propose the matter, as most to his advantage, and then it will be enough for him to say: "I ask for a certain sum of money due to me according to agreement; I ask for what was bequeathed to me by will." It is the defendant's business to show that he has no right to such a debt or legacy. On other occasions it is enough, and more advisable, for the plaintiff to point out merely the fact: "I say that Horatius killed his sister." This simple proposition makes known the whole crime, but the details and the cause of the fact will suit better the defendant. Let it be supposed, on the other hand, that the fact can not be denied or excused; then the defendant, instead of narrating, will best abide by the question of right. Some one is accused of sacrilege for stealing the money of a private person out of a temple. The pleader of the cause had better confess the fact than give an account of it. "We do not deny that this money was taken out of the temple. It was the money of a private person, and not set apart for any religious use. But the plaintiff calumniates us by an action for sacrilege. It is, therefore, your business, gentlemen, to decide whether it can properly be specified as sacrilege."

THE TWO KINDS OF NARRATION

There are two kinds of narration in judicial matters, the one for the cause, the other for things belonging to it. "I have not killed that man." This needs no narration. I admit it does not; but there may be a narration, and even somewhat long, concerning the probable causes of innocence in the accused, as his former integrity of life, the opponent's motives for endangering the life of a guiltless person, and other circumstances arguing the incredibility of the accusation. The accuser does not merely say, "You have committed that murder," but shows reasons to evince its credibility; as, in tragedies, when Teucer imputes the death of Ajax to Ulysses, he says that "He was found in a lonely place, near the dead body of his enemy, with his sword all bloody." Ulysses, in answer, not only denies the crime, but protests there was no enmity between him and Ajax, and that they never contended but for glory. Then he relates how he came into that solitary place, how he found Ajax dead, and that it was Ajax's own sword he drew out of his wound. To these are subjoined proofs, but the proofs, too, are not without narration, the plaintiff alleging, "You were in the place where your enemy was found killed." "I was not," says the defendant, and he tells where he was.

HOW TO MAKE THE CONCLUSION

The end of the narration is rather more for persuading than informing. When, therefore, the judges might not require information, yet, if we consider it advisable to draw them over to our way of thinking, we may relate the matter with certain precautions, as, that tho they have knowledge of the affair in general, still would it not be amiss if they chose to examine into every particular fact as it happened. Sometimes we may diversify the exposition with a variety of figures and turns; as, "You remember"; "Perhaps it would be unnecessary to insist any longer on this point"; "But why should I speak further when you are so well acquainted with the matter."

A subject of frequent discussion is to know whether the narration ought immediately to follow the exordium. They who think it should, seem to have some reason on their side, for as the design of the exordium is to dispose the judges to hear us with all the good will, docility, and attention, we wish, and as arguments can have no effect without previous knowledge of the cause, it follows naturally that they should have this knowledge as soon as it can conveniently be given to them.

PURPOSES OF THE NARRATION

If the narration be entirely for us, we may content ourselves with those three parts, whereby the judge is made the more easily to understand, remember, and believe. But let none think of finding fault if I require the narration which is entirely for us, to be probable tho true, for many things are true but scarcely credible, as, on the contrary, many things are false tho frequently probable. We ought, therefore, to be careful that the judge should believe as much what we pretend as the truth we say, by preserving in both a probability to be credited.

Those three qualities of the narration belong in like manner to all other parts of the discourse, for obscurity must be avoided throughout, and we must everywhere keep within certain bounds, and all that is said must be probable; but a strict observance of these particulars ought to be kept more especially in that part wherein the judge receives his first information, for if there it should happen that he either does not understand, remember, or believe, our labor in all other parts will be to no purpose.

THE QUALITIES NEEDED FOR SUCCESS

The narration will be clear and intelligible if, first, it be expressed in proper and significant words, which have nothing mean and low, nothing far-fetched, and nothing uncommon. Second, if it distinguishes exactly things, persons, times, places, causes; all of which should be accompanied with a suitable delivery, that the judge may retain the more easily what is said.

This is a quality neglected by most of our orators, who, charmed by the applause of a rabble brought together by chance, or even bribed to applaud with admiration every word and period, can neither endure the attentive silence of a judicious audience, nor seem to themselves to be eloquent unless they make everything ring about them with tumultuous clamor. To explain simply the fact, appears to them too low, and common, and too much within the reach of the illiterate, but I fancy that what they despise as easy is not so much because of inclination as because of inability to effect it. For the more experience we have, the more we find that nothing else is so difficult as to speak in such a manner that all who have heard us may think they could acquit themselves equally as well. The reason for the contrary notion is that what is so said is considered as merely true and not as fine and beautiful. But will not the orator express himself in the most perfect manner, when he seems to speak truth? Now, indeed, the narration is laid out as a champion-ground for eloquence to display itself in; the voice, the gesture, the thoughts, the expression, are all worked up to a pitch of extravagance, and what is monstrous, the action is applauded, and yet the cause is far from being understood. But we shall forego further reflections on this misguided notion, lest we offend more by reproving faults, than gratify by giving advice.

The narration will have its due brevity if we begin by explaining the affair from the point where it is of concern to the judge; next, if we say nothing foreign to the cause; and last, if we avoid all superfluities, yet without curtailing anything that may give insight into the cause or be to its advantage. There is a certain brevity of parts, however, which makes a long whole: "I came to the harbor, I saw a ship ready for sailing, I asked the price for passengers, I agreed as to what I should give, I went aboard, we weighed anchor, we cleared the coast, and sailed on briskly." None of these circumstances could be exprest in fewer words, but it is sufficient to say, "I sailed from the port." And as often as the end of a thing sufficiently denotes what went before, we may rest satisfied with it as facilitating the understanding of all other circumstances.

But often when striving to be short, we become obscure, a fault equally to be avoided, therefore it is better that the narration should have a little too much, than that it should lack enough. What is redundant, disgusts; what is necessary is cut down with danger. I would not have this rule restricted to what is barely sufficient for pronouncing judgment on, because the narration may be concise, yet not, on that account, be without ornament. In such cases it would appear as coming from an illiterate person. Pleasure, indeed, has a secret charm; and the things which please seem less tedious. A pleasant and smooth road, tho it be longer, fatigues less than a rugged and disagreeable short cut. I am not so fond of conciseness as not to make room for brightening a narration with proper embellishments. If quite homely and curtailed on all sides, it will be not so much a narration as a poor huddling up of things together.

GETTING YOUR STATEMENTS ACCEPTED

The best way to make the narration probable is to first consult with ourselves on whatever is agreeable to nature, that nothing may be said contrary to it; next, to find causes and reasons for facts, not for all, but for those belonging to the question; and last, to have characters answerable to the alleged facts which we would have believed; as, if one were guilty of theft, we should represent him as a miser; of adultery, as addicted to impure lusts; of manslaughter, as hot and rash. The contrary takes place in defense, and the facts must agree with time, place, and the like.

Sometimes a cause may be prepared by a proposition, and afterward narrated. All circumstances are unfavorable to three sons who have conspired against their father's life. They cast lots who shall strike the blow. He on whom the lot falls, enters his father's bed-chamber at night, with a poniard, but has not courage to put the design into execution. The second and the third do the same. The father wakes. All confess their wicked purpose, and by virtue of a law made and provided for such case, they are to be disinherited. But should the father, who has already made a partition of his estate in their favor, plead their cause, he may proceed thus: "Children are accused of parricide, whose father is still alive, and they are sued in consequence of a law that is not properly applicable to their case. I need not here give an account of a transaction that is foreign to the point of law in question. But if you require a confession of my guilt, I have been a hard father to them, and rather too much occupied in hoarding up the income of my estate, which would have been better spent in necessaries for them." Afterward he may say that they did not form this plan by themselves, that they were instigated to it by others who had more indulgent parents, that the result clearly showed they were not capable of so unnatural an action, that there was no necessity for binding themselves by oath if in reality they could have had such an inclination, nor of casting lots if each did not want to avoid the perpetration of such a crime. All these circumstances, such as they are, will be favorably received, softened in some measure by the short defense of the previous propositions.

THE ORDER OF THE NARRATION

I am not of the opinion of those who think that the facts ought always to be related in the same order in which they happened. That manner of narration is best which is of most advantage to the cause, and it may, not improperly, call in the aid of a diversity of figures. Sometimes we may pretend that a thing has been overlooked, so that it may be better exprest elsewhere than it would be in its own order and place; assuring the judges at the same time that we shall resume the proper order, but that the cause in this way will be better understood. Sometimes, after explaining the whole affair, we may subjoin the antecedent causes. And thus it is that the art of defense, not circumscribed by any one invariable rule, must be adapted to the nature and circumstances of the cause.

It will not be amiss to intimate that nothing enhances so much the credibility of a narration as the authority of him who makes it, and this authority it is our duty to acquire, above all, by an irreproachable life, and next, by the manner of enforcing it. The more grave and serious it is, the more weight it will have. Here all suspicion of cunning and artifice should, therefore, be particularly avoided, for the judges, ever distrustful, are here principally on their guard, and, likewise, nothing should seem a pure fiction, or the work of study, which all might rather be believed to proceed from the cause than the orator. But this we can not endure, and we think our art lost unless it is seen; whereas it ceases to be art if it is seen.

DIVISION AND ARGUMENT

Some are of the opinion that division should always be used, as by it the cause will be more clear and the judge more attentive and more easily taught when he knows of what we speak to him and of what we intend afterward to speak. Others think this is attended with danger to the orator, either by his sometimes forgetting what he has promised, or by something else occurring to the judge or auditor, which he did not think of in the division. I can not well imagine how this may happen, unless with one who is either destitute of sense or rash enough to plead without preparation. In any other respect, nothing else can set a subject in so clear a light as just division. It is a means to which we are directed by the guidance of nature, because keeping in sight the heads on which we propose to speak, is the greatest help the memory can have.

THE MISTAKE OF TOO MANY DIVISIONS

But if division should seem requisite, I am not inclined to assent to the notion of those who would have it extend to more than three parts. Indeed, when the parts are too many, they escape the judge's memory and distract his attention; but a cause is not scrupulously to be tied down to this number, as it may require more.

DISADVANTAGES OF DIVISIONS

There are reasons for not always using division, the principal reason being that most things are better received when seemingly of extempore invention and not suggestive of study, but arising in the pleading from the nature of the thing itself. Whence such figures are not unpleasing as, "I had almost forgotten to say"; "It escaped my memory to acquaint you"; and "You have given me a good hint." For if the proofs should be proposed without something of a reputation of this kind, they would lose, in the sequel, all the graces of novelty.

The distinguishing of questions, and the discussing of them, should be equally avoided. But the listeners' passions ought to be excited, and their attention diverted from its former bias, for it is the orator's business not so much to instruct as to enforce his eloquence by emotion, to which nothing can be more contrary than minute and scrupulously exact division of a discourse into parts.

WHEN THE DIVISION IS DESIRABLE

If many things are to be avoided or refuted, the division will be both useful and pleasing, causing everything to appear in the order in which it is to be said. But if we defend a single crime by various ways, division will be superfluous, as, "I shall make it clear that the person I defend is not such as to make it seem probable that he could be guilty of murder; it shall also be shown that he had no motives to induce him to do it; and lastly, that he was across the sea when this murder took place." Whatever is cited and argued before the third point must seem quite unnecessary, for the judge is in haste to have you come to that which is of most consequence, and the patient, will tacitly call upon you to acquit yourself of your promise, or, if he has much business to dispatch, or his dignity puts him above your trifling, or he is of a peevish humor, he will oblige you to speak to the purpose, and perhaps do so in disrespectful terms.

PITFALLS IN ARGUMENT

Many doubt the desirability of this kind of defense: "If I had killed him, I should have done well; but I did not kill him." Where is the occasion, say they, for the first proposition if the second be true? They run counter to each other, and whoever advances both, will be credited in neither. This is partly true, for if the last proposition be unquestionable, it is the only one that should be used. But if we are apprehensive of anything in the stronger, we may use both. On these occasions persons seem to be differently affected; one will believe the fact, and exculpate the right; another will condemn the right, and perhaps not credit the fact. So, one dart may be enough for an unerring hand to hit the mark, but chance and many darts must effect the same result for an uncertain aim. Cicero clears up this matter in his defense of Milo. He first shows Clodius to be the aggressor, and then, by a superabundance of right, adds that tho he might not be the aggressor, it was brave and glorious in Milo to have delivered Rome of so bad a citizen.

Tho division may not always be necessary, yet when properly used it gives great light and beauty to a discourse. This it effects not only by adding more perspicuity to what is said, but also by refreshing the minds of the hearers by a view of each part circumscribed within its bounds; just so milestones ease in some measure the fatigue of travelers, it being a pleasure to know the extent of the labor they have undergone, and to know what remains encourages them to persevere, as a thing does not necessarily seem long when there is a certainty of coming to the end.

ESSENTIALS OF GOOD ARGUMENT

Every division, therefore, when it may be employed to advantage, ought to be first clear and intelligible, for what is worse than being obscure in a thing, the use of which is to guard against obscurity in other things? Second, it ought to be short, and not encumbered with any superfluous word, because we do not enter upon the subject matter, but only point it out.

If proofs be strong and cogent, they should be proposed and insisted on separately; if weak, it will be best to collect them into a body. In the first case, being persuasive by themselves, it would be improper to obscure them by the confusion of others: they should appear in their due light. In the second case, being naturally weak, they should be made to support each other. If, therefore, they are not greatly effective in point of quality, they may be in that of number, all of them having a tendency to prove the same thing; as, if one were accused of killing another for the sake of inheriting his fortune: "You did expect an inheritance, and it was something very considerable; you were poor, and your creditors troubled you more than ever; you also offended him who had appointed you his heir, and you know that he intended to alter his will." These proofs taken separately are of little moment, and common; but collectively their shock is felt, not as a peal of thunder, but as a shower of hail.

The judge's memory, however, is not always to be loaded with the arguments we may invent. They will create disgust, and beget distrust in him, as he can not think such arguments to be powerful enough which we ourselves do not think sufficient. But to go on arguing and proving, in the case of self-evident things, would be a piece of folly not unlike that of bringing a candle to light us when the sun is in its greatest splendor.

To these some add proofs which they call moral, drawn from the milder passions; and the most powerful, in the opinion of Aristotle, are such as arise from the person of him who speaks, if he be a man of real integrity. This is a primary consideration; and a secondary one, remote, indeed, yet following, will be the probable notion entertained of his irreproachable life.

THE BEST ORDER OF THE ARGUMENT

It has been a matter of debate, also, whether the strongest proofs should have place in the beginning, to make an immediate impression on the hearers, or at the end, to make the impression lasting with them, or to distribute them, partly in the beginning and partly at the end, placing the weaker in the middle, or to begin with the weakest and proceed to the strongest. For my part I think this should depend on the nature and exigencies of the cause, yet with this reservation, that the discourse might not dwindle from the powerful into what is nugatory and frivolous.

Let the young orator, for whose instruction I make these remarks, accustom himself as much as possible to copy nature and truth. As in schools he often engages in sham battles, in imitation of the contests of the bar, let him even then have an eye to victory, and learn to strike home, dealing moral blows and putting himself on his defense as if really in earnest. It is the master's business to require this duty, and to commend it according as it is well executed. For if they love praise to the degree of seeking it in their faults, which does them much harm, they will desire it more passionately when they know it to be the reward of real merit. The misfortune now is that they commonly pass over necessary things in silence, considering what is for the good of the cause as of little or no account if it be not conducive to the embellishment of the discourse.

THE PERORATION

The peroration, called by some the completion, by others the conclusion, of a discourse, is of two kinds, and regards either the matters discust in it or the moving of the passions.

The repetition of the matter and the collecting it together, which is called by the Greeks recapitulation, and by some of the Latins enumeration, serves for refreshing the judge's memory, for placing the whole cause in one direct point of view, and for enforcing in a body many proofs which, separately, made less impression. It would seem that this repetition ought to be very short, and the Greek term sufficiently denotes that we ought to run over only the principal heads, for if we are long in doing it, it will not be an enumeration that we make, but, as it were, a second discourse. The points which may seem to require this enumeration, however, ought to be pronounced with some emphasis, and enlivened with opposite thoughts, and diversified by figures, otherwise nothing will be more disagreeable than a mere cursory repetition, which would seem to show distrust of the judge's memory.

RULES FOR THE PERORATION

This seems to be the only kind of peroration allowed by most of the Athenians and by almost all the philosophers who left anything written on the art of oratory. The Athenians, I suppose, were of that opinion because it was customary at Athens to silence, by the public crier, any orator who should attempt to move the passions. I am less surprized at this opinion among philosophers, every perturbation of the mind being considered by them as vicious; nor did it seem to them compatible with sound morality to divert the judge from truth, nor agreeable to the idea of an honest man to have recourse to any sinister stratagem. Yet moving the passions will be acknowledged necessary when truth and justice can not be otherwise obtained and when public good is concerned in the decision. All agree that recapitulation may also be employed to advantage in other parts of the pleading, if the cause is complicated and requires many arguments to defend it, and, on the other hand, it will admit of no doubt that many causes are so short and simple as to have no occasion in any part of them for recapitulation. The above rules for the peroration apply equally to the accuser and to the defendant's advocate.

They, likewise, use nearly the same passions, but the accuser more seldom and more sparingly, and the defendant oftener and with greater emotions; for it is the business of the former to stir up aversion, indignation, and other similar passions in the minds of the judges, and of the latter to bend their hearts to compassion. Yet the accuser is sometimes not without tears, in deploring the distress of those in whose behalf he sues for satisfaction, and the defendant sometimes complains with great vehemence of the persecution raised against him by the calumnies and conspiracy of his enemies. It would be best, therefore, to distinguish and discuss separately the different passions excited on the parts of the plaintiff and defendant, which are most commonly, as I have said, very like what takes place in the exordium, but are treated in a freer and fuller manner in the peroration.

PURPOSES OF THE PERORATION

The favor of the judges toward us is more sparingly sued for in the beginning, it being then sufficient to gain their attention, as the whole discourse remains in which to make further impressions. But in the peroration we must strive to bring the judge into that disposition of the mind which it is necessary for us that he should retain when he comes to pass judgment. The peroration being finished, we can say no more, nor can anything be reserved for another place. Both of the contending sides, therefore, try to conciliate the judge, to make him unfavorable to the opponent, to rouse and occasionally allay his passions; and both may find their method of procedure in this short rule, which is, to keep in view the whole stress of the cause, and finding what it contains that is favorable, odious, or deplorable, in reality or in probability, to say those things which would make the greatest impression on themselves if they sat as judges.

I have already mentioned in the rules for the exordium how the accuser might conciliate the judges. Yet some things, which it was enough to point out there, should be wrought to a fulness in the peroration, especially if the pleading be against some one universally hated, and a common disturber, and if the condemnation of the culprit should redound as much to the honor of the judges as his acquittal to their shame. Thus Calvus spoke admirably against Vatinius:

"You know, good sirs, that Vatinius is guilty, and no one is unaware that you know it." Cicero, in the same way, informs the judges that if anything is capable of reestablishing the reputation of their judgment, it must be the condemnation of Verres. If it be proper to intimidate the judges, as Cicero likewise does, against Verres, this is done with better effect in the peroration than in the exordium. I have already explained my sentiments on this point.

HOW TO AROUSE EMOTIONS

In short, when it is requisite to excite envy, hatred, or indignation there is greater scope for doing this to advantage in the peroration than elsewhere. The interest in the accused may naturally excite the judge's envy, the infamy of his crimes may draw upon him his hatred, the little respect he shows him may rouse his indignation. If he is stubborn, haughty, presumptuous, let him be painted in all the glaring colors that aggravate such vicious temper, and these manifested not only from his words and deeds, but from face, manner, and dress. I remember, on my first coming to the bar, a shrewd remark of the accuser of Cossutianus Capito. He pleaded in Greek before the Emperor, but the meaning of his words was: "Might it not be said that this man disdains even to respect Cæsar."

The accuser has recourse frequently to the arousing of compassion, either by setting forth the distrest state of him for whom he hopes to find redress, or by describing the desolation and ruin into which his children and relations are likely thereby to be involved. He may, too, move the judges by holding out to them a prospect of what may happen hereafter if injuries and violence remain unpunished, the consequence of which will be that either his client must abandon his dwelling and the care of his effects, or must resolve to endure patiently all the injustice his enemy may try to do him.

The accuser more frequently will endeavor to caution the judge against the pity with which the defendant intends to inspire him, and he will stimulate him, in as great a degree as he can, to judge according to his conscience. Here, too, will be the place to anticipate whatever it is thought the opponent may do or say, for it makes the judges more circumspect regarding the sacredness of their oath, and by it the answer to the pleading may lose the indulgence which it is expected to receive, together with the charm of novelty in all the particulars which the accuser has already cleared up. The judges, besides, may be informed of the answer they should make to those who might threaten to have their sentence reversed; and this is another kind of recapitulation.

The persons concerned are very proper objects for affecting the mind of the judge, for the judge does not seem to himself to hear so much the orator weeping over others' misfortunes, as he imagines his ears are smitten with the feelings and voice of the distrest. Even their dumb appearance might be a sufficiently moving language to draw tears, and as their wretchedness would appear in lively colors if they were to speak it themselves, so proportionately it must be thought to have a powerful effect when exprest, as it were, from their own mouths. Just so, in theatrical representations, the same voice, and the same emphatic pronunciation, become very interesting under the masks used for personating different characters. With a like view Cicero, tho he gives not the voice of a suppliant to Milo, but, on the contrary, commends his unshaken constancy, yet does he adapt to him words and complaints not unworthy of a man of spirit: "O my labors, to no purpose undertaken! Deceiving hopes! Useless projects!"

This exciting of pity, however, should never be long, it being said, not without reason, that "nothing dries up so soon as tears." If time can mitigate the pangs of real grief, of course the counterfeit grief assumed in speaking must sooner vanish; so that if we dally, the auditor finding himself overcharged with mournful thoughts, tries to resume his tranquility, and thus ridding himself of the emotion that overpowered him, soon returns to the exercise of cool reason. We must, therefore, never allow this kind of emotion to become languid, but when we have wound up the passions to their greatest height, we must instantly drop the subject, and not expect that any one will long bewail another's mishap. Therefore, as in other parts, the discourse should be well supported, and rather rise, so here particularly it should grow to its full vigor, because that which makes no addition to what has already been said seems to diminish it, and a passion soon evaporates that once begins to subside.

Tears are excited not only by words but by doing certain things, whence it is not unusual to present the very persons who are in danger of condemnation, in a garb suitable to their distress, together with their children and relations. Accusers, too, make it a custom to show a bloody sword, fractured bones picked out of wounds, and garments drenched in blood. Sometime, likewise, they unbind wounds to show their condition, and strip bodies naked to show the stripes they have received. These acts are commonly of mighty efficacy, as fully revealing the reality of the occurrence. Thus it was that Cæsar's robe, bloody all over, exposed in the Forum, drove the people of Rome into an excess of madness. It was well known that he was assassinated; his body also lay in state, until his funeral should take place; yet that garment, still dripping with blood, formed so graphic a picture of the horrible murder that it seemed to them to have been perpetrated that very instant.

It will not be amiss to hint that the success of the peroration depends much on the manner of the parties in conforming themselves to the emotions and action of their advocates. Stupidity, rusticity, and a want of sensibility and attention, as it is said, throw cold water on a cause against which the orator can not be too well provided. I have, indeed, often seen them act quite contrary to their advocate's instructions. Not the least show of concern could be observed in their countenance. They laughed foolishly and without reason, and made others laugh by some ridiculous gesticulation or grimace, especially when the heat of a debate exhibited anything akin to theatrical action.

An orator of slender ability will acquit himself better if he allows the judges by themselves to feel the compassion with which his subject may naturally inspire them, especially since the appearance, and voice, and studied air of the advocate's countenance are often ridiculed by such as are not affected by them. Let the orator make an exact estimate of his powers, therefore, and be conscious of the burden he undertakes. Here there is no middle state; he must either make his hearers weep, or expect to be laughed at.

It should not be imagined, as some have thought, that all exciting of the passions, all sentimental emotions, ought to be confined to the exordium and peroration. In them they are most frequent, yet other parts admit them likewise, but in a shorter compass, as their greatest stress should be reserved for the end. For here, if anywhere, the orator may be allowed to open all the streams of eloquence. If we have executed all other parts to advantage, here we take possession of the minds of the judges, and having escaped all rocks, may expand all our sails for a favorable gale; and as amplification makes a great part of the peroration, we then may raise and embellish our style with the choicest expressions and brightest thoughts. And, indeed, the conclusion of a speech should bear some resemblance to that of tragedy and comedy, wherein the actor courts the spectator's applause. In other parts the passions may be touched upon, as they naturally rise out of the subject, and no horrible or sorrowful thing should be set forth without accompanying it with a suitable sentiment. When the debate may be on the quality of a thing, it is properly subjoined to the proofs of each thing brought out. When we plead a cause complicated with a variety of circumstances, then it will be necessary to use many perorations, as it were; as Cicero does against Verres, lending his tears occasionally to Philodamus, to the masters of ships, to the crucified Roman citizens, and to many others.

PASSION AND PERSUASION

It may well be imagined that nothing else is so important in the whole art of oratory as the proper use of the passions. A slender genius, aided by learning or experience, may be sufficient to manage certain parts to some advantage, yet I think they are fit only for instructing the judges, and as masters and models for those who take no concern beyond passing for good speakers. But to possess the secret of forcibly carrying away the judges, of moving them, as we please, to a certain disposition of mind, of inflaming them with anger, of softening them to pity, so as to draw tears from them, all this is rare, tho by it the orator is made most distinguished and by it eloquence gains empire over hearts. The cause itself is naturally productive of arguments, and the better share generally falls to the lot of the more rightful side of the question, so that whichever side wins by dint of argument, may think that so far they did not lack an advocate. But when violence is to be used to influence the minds of the judges, when they are to be turned from coolly reflecting on the truth that works against us, then comes the true exercise of the orator's powers; and this is what the contending parties can not inform us of, nor is it contained in the state of their cases. Proofs, it is true, make the judges presume that our cause is the better, but passion makes them wish it to be such, and as they wish it, they are not far from believing it to be so. For as soon as they begin to absorb from us our passions of anger, favor, hatred, or pity, they make the affair their own. As lovers can not be competent judges of beauty, because love blinds them, so here a judge attentive to the tumultuous working of a passion, loses sight of the way by which he should proceed to inquire after the truth. The impetuous torrent sweeps him away, and he is borne down in the current. The effect of arguments and witnesses is not known until judgment has been passed, but the judge who has been affected by the orator, still sitting and hearing, declares his real sentiments. Has not he who is seen to melt into tears, already pronounced sentence? Such, then, is the power of moving the passions, to which the orator ought to direct all his efforts, this being his principal work and labor, since without it all other resources are naked, hungry, weak, and unpleasing. The passions are the very life and soul of persuasion.

QUALITIES NEEDED IN THE ORATOR

What we require in the orator is, in general, a character of goodness, not only mild and pleasing, but humane, insinuating, amiable, and charming to the hearer; and its greatest perfection will be if all, as influenced by it, shall seem to flow from the nature of things and persons, that so the morals of the orator may shine forth from his discourse and be known in their genuine colors. This character of goodness should invariably be maintained by those whom a mutual tie ought to bind in strict union, whenever it may happen that they suffer anything from each other, or pardon, or make satisfaction, or admonish, or reprimand, but far from betraying any real anger or hatred.

A sentiment very powerful for exciting hatred may arise when an act of submission to our opponents is understood as a silent reproach of their insolence. Our willingness to yield must indeed show them to be insupportable and troublesome, and it commonly happens that they who have desire for railing, and are too free and hot in their invectives, do not imagine that the jealousy they create is of far greater prejudice to them than the malice of their speech.

All this presupposes that the orator himself ought to be a good and humane man. The virtues which he commends, if he possibly can, in his client, he should possess, or be supposed to possess, himself. In this way will he be of singular advantage to the cause he undertakes, the good opinion he has created of himself being a prejudice in its favor. For if while he speaks he appears to be a bad man, he must in consequence plead ill, because what he says will be thought repugnant to justice. The style and manner suitable on these occasions ought, therefore, to be sweet and insinuating, never hot and imperious, never hazarded in too elevated a strain. It will be sufficient to speak in a proper, pleasing, and probable way.

The orator's business in regard to the passions should be not only to paint atrocious and lamentable things as they are, but even to make those seem grievous which are considered tolerable, as when we say that an injurious word is less pardonable than a blow, and that death is preferable to dishonor. For the powers of eloquence do not consist so much in forcing the judge into sentiments which the nature of the matter itself may be sufficient to inspire him with, as they do in producing and creating, as it were, the same sentiments when the subject may seem not to admit them. This is the vehemence of oratorical ability which knows how to equal and even to surpass the enormity and indignity of the facts it exposes, a quality of singular consequence to the orator, and one in which Demosthenes excelled all others.

THE SECRET OF MOVING THE PASSIONS

The great secret for moving the passions is to be moved ourselves, for the imitation of grief, anger, indignation, will often be ridiculous if conforming to only our words and countenance, while our heart at the same time is estranged from them. What other reason makes the afflicted exclaim in so eloquent a manner during the first transports of their grief? And how, otherwise, do the most ignorant speak eloquently in anger, unless it be from this force and these mental feelings?

In such passions, therefore, which we would represent as true copies of real ones, let us be ourselves like those who unfeignedly suffer, and let our speech proceed from such a disposition of mind as that in which we would have the judge be. Will he grieve who hears me speak with an expressionless face and air of indifference? Will he be angry when I, who am to excite him to anger, remain cool and sedate? Will he shed tears when I plead unconcerned? All this is attempting impossibilities. Nothing warms nor moistens but that which is endued with the quality of heat or moisture, nor does anything give to another a color it has not itself. The principal consideration, then, must be that we, ourselves, retain the impression of which we would have the judges susceptible, and be ourselves affected before we endeavor to affect others.

THE POWER OF MENTAL IMAGERY

But how shall we be affected, the emotions or passions being not at our command? This may be done by what we may call visions, whereby the images of things absent are so represented to the mind that we seem to see them with our eyes and have them present before us. Whoever can work up his imagination to an intuitive view of this kind, will be very successful in moving the passions.

If I deplore the fate of a man who has been assassinated, may I not paint in my mind a lively picture of all that probably happened on the occasion? Shall not the assassin appear to rush forth suddenly from his lurking place? Shall not the other appear seized with horror? Shall he not cry out, beg for his life, or fly to save it? Shall I not see the assassin dealing the deadly blow, and the defenseless wretch falling dead at his feet? Shall I not picture vividly in my mind the blood gushing from his wounds, his ghastly face, his groans, and the last gasp he fetches?

When there is occasion for moving to compassion, we should believe and, indeed, be persuaded that the distress and misfortunes of which we speak have happened to ourselves. Let us place ourselves in the very position of those for whom we feel sorrow on account of their having suffered such grievous and unmerited treatment. Let us plead their cause, not as if it were another's, but taking to ourselves, for a short time, their whole grief. In this way we shall speak as if the case were our own. I have seen comedians who, when they have just appeared in a mournful character, often make their exit with tears in their eyes. If, then, the expression given to imaginary passions can affect so powerfully, what should not orators do, whose inner feelings ought to sympathize with their manner of speaking, which can not happen unless they are truly affected by the danger to which their clients are exposed.

RULES FOR PRACTISE

In the declamatory exercises of schools it would be expedient, likewise, to move the passions and imagine the scene as a real one in life, and it is the more important as there the part is performed rather of a pleader against some person, than an advocate for some person. We represent a person who has lost his children, or has been shipwrecked, or is in danger of losing his life, but of what significance is it to personate such characters, unless we also assume their real sentiments. This nature, and these properties of the passions, I thought it incumbent on me not to conceal from the reader, for I, myself, such as I am, or have been (for I flatter myself that I have acquired some reputation at the bar), have often been so affected that not only tears, but even paleness, and grief, not unlike that which is real, have betrayed my emotions.

THE STUDY OF WORDS

What now follows requires special labor and care, the purpose being to treat of elocution, which in the opinion of all orators is the most difficult part of our work, for M. Antonius says that he has seen many good speakers, but none eloquent. He thinks it good enough for a speaker to say whatever is necessary on a subject, but only the most eloquent may discuss it with grace and elegance. If down to the time he lived in, this perfection was not discoverable in any orator, and neither in himself nor in L. Crassus, it is certain that it was lacking in them and their predecessors only on account of its extreme difficulty. Cicero says that invention and disposition show the man of sense, but eloquence the orator. He therefore took particular pains about the rules for this part, and that he had reason for so doing the very name of eloquence sufficiently declares. For to be eloquent is nothing else than to be able to set forth all the lively images you have conceived in your mind, and to convey them to the hearers in the same rich coloring, without which all the principles we have laid down are useless, and are like a sword concealed and kept sheathed in its scabbard.

This, then, is what we are principally to learn; this is what we can not attain without the help of art; this ought to be the object of our study, our exercise, our imitation; this may be full employment for our whole life; by this, one orator excels another; and from this proceeds diversity of style.

THE PROPER VALUE OF WORDS

It should not be inferred from what is said here that all our care must be about words. On the contrary, to such as would abuse this concession of mine, I declare positively my disapprobation of those persons who, neglecting things, the nerves of causes, consume themselves in a frivolous study about words. This they do for the sake of elegance, which indeed is a fine quality when natural but not when affected. Sound bodies, with a healthy condition of blood, and strong by exercise, receive their beauty from the very things from which they receive their strength. They are fresh-colored, active, and supple, neither too much nor too little in flesh. Paint and polish them with feminine cosmetics, and admiration ceases; the very pains taken to make them appear more beautiful add to the dislike we conceive for them. Yet a magnificent, and suitable, dress adds authority to man; but an effeminate dress, the garb of luxury and softness, lays open the corruption of the heart without adding to the ornament of the body. In like manner, translucent and flashy elocution weakens the things it clothes. I would, therefore, recommend care about words, but solicitude about things.

The choicest expressions are for the most part inherent in things, and are seen in their own light, but we search after them as if always hiding and stealing themselves away from us. Thus we never think that what ought to be said is at hand; we fetch it from afar, and force our invention. Eloquence requires a more manly temper, and if its whole body be sound and vigorous, it is quite regardless of the nicety of paring the nails and adjusting the hair.

THE DANGER OF VERBIAGE

It often happens, too, that an oration becomes worse by attending to these niceties, because simplicity, the language of truth, is its greatest ornament, and affectation the reverse. The expressions that show care, and would also appear as newly formed, fine, and eloquent, lose the graces at which they aim, and are far from being striking and well received, because they obscure the sense by spreading a sort of shadow about it, or by being too crowded they choke it up, like thick-sown grain that must run up too spindling. That which may be spoken in a plain, direct manner we express by paraphrase; and we use repetitions where to say a thing once is enough; and what is well signified by one word, we load with many, and most things we choose to signify rather by circumlocution than by proper and pertinent terms.

A proper word, indeed, now has no charms, nothing appearing to us fine which might have been said by another word. We borrow metaphors from the whims and conceits of the most extravagant poets, and we fancy ourselves exceedingly witty, when others must have a good deal of wit to understand us. Cicero is explicit in his views in this respect. "The greatest fault a speech can have," says he, "is when it departs from the common way of discourse and the custom of common sense." But Cicero would pass for a harsh and barbarous author, compared to us, who make little of whatever nature dictates, who seek not ornaments, but delicacies and refinements, as if there were any beauty in words without an agreement with things, for if we were to labor throughout our whole life in consulting their propriety, clearness, ornament, and due placing, we should lose the whole fruit of our studies.

ACQUIRING A PRACTICAL VOCABULARY

Yet many are seen to hesitate at single words, even while they invent, and reflect on and measure what they invent. If this were done designedly to use always the best, this unhappy temper would still be detestable, as it must check the course of speaking and extinguish the heat of thought by delay and diffidence. For the orator is wretched, and, I may say, poor, who can not patiently lose a word. But he will lose none who first has studied a good manner of speaking, and by reading well the best authors has furnished himself with a copious supply of words and made himself expert in the art of placing them. Much practise will so improve him afterward that he always will have them at hand and ready for use, the thought fitting in naturally with the proper manner of expression.

But all this requires previous study, an acquired faculty, and a rich fund of words. For solicitude in regard to inventing, judging, and comparing, should take place when we learn, and not when we speak. Otherwise they who have not sufficiently cultivated their talents for speaking will experience the fate of those who have made no provision for the future. But if a proper stock of words is already prepared, they will attend as in duty bound, not so much in the way of answering exigencies as always to seem inherent in the thought and to follow as a shadow does a body.

HOW TO CHOOSE THE RIGHT WORDS

Yet this care should not exceed its due bounds, for when words are authorized by use, are significant, elegant, and aptly placed, what more need we trouble ourselves about? But some eternally will find fault, and almost scan every syllable, who, even when they have found what is best, seek after something that is more ancient, remote, and unexpected, not understanding that the thought must suffer in a discourse, and can have nothing of value, where only the words are commendable. Let us, therefore, pay particular regard to elocution, yet, at the same time be convinced that nothing is to be done for the sake of words, they having been invented solely for the sake of things. The most proper words always will be those which are best expressive of the ideas in our mind, and which produce in the ideas of the judges the effect we desire. Such undoubtedly will make a speech both admirable and pleasing, but not so admirable as are prodigies, nor pleasing by a vicious and unseemly pleasure, but a pleasure reflecting dignity with praise.

ELEGANCE AND GRACE

The orator will recommend himself particularly by the embellishments he adopts, securing in other ways the approbation of the learned, and in this also the favor of popular applause.

Not so much with strong as with shining armor did Cicero engage in the cause of Cornelius. His success was not due merely to instructing the judges, and speaking in a pure and clear style. These qualities would not have brought him the honor of the admiration and applause of the Roman people. It was the sublimity, magnificence, splendor, and dignity of his eloquence that forced from them signal demonstrations of their amazement. Nor would such unusual eulogies have been given him if his speech had contained nothing extraordinary, nothing but what was common. And, indeed, I believe that those present were not completely aware of what they were doing, and that what they did was neither spontaneous, nor from an act of judgment, but that filled with a sort of enthusiasm, and not considering the place they were in, they burst forth with unrestrained excitement.

THE VALUE OF BEAUTY OF EXPRESSION

These ornaments of speech, therefore, may be thought to contribute not a little to the success of a cause, for they who hear willingly are more attentive and more disposed to believe. Most commonly it is pleasure that wins them over, and sometimes they are seized and carried away with admiration. A glittering sword strikes the eyes with some terror, and thunder would not so shock us if its crash only, and not its lightning, was dreaded. Therefore Cicero, with good reason, says in one of his epistles to Brutus: "The eloquence which does not excite admiration, I regard as nothing." Aristotle, too, would have us endeavor to attain this perfection.

But this embellishment, I must again and again repeat, ought to be manly, noble, and modest; neither inclining to effeminate delicacy, nor assuming a color indebted to paint, but glistening with health and spirits.

Let none of those who build up their reputation on a corrupt manner of eloquence, say that I am an enemy to such as speak with elegance. I do not deny that it is a perfection, but I do not ascribe it to them. Shall I think a piece of ground better laid out and improved, in which one shall show me lilies and violets and pleasing cascades, than one where there is a full harvest or vines laden with grapes? Shall I esteem a barren planetree and shorn myrtles beyond the fruitful olive and the elm courting the embraces of the vine? The rich may pride themselves on these pleasures of the eye, but how little would be their value if they had nothing else?

But shall no beauty, no symmetry, be observed in the care of fruit trees? Undoubtedly there should, and I would place them in a certain order, and keep a due distance in planting them. What is more beautiful than the quincunx, which, whatever way you look, retains the same direct position? Planting them out so will also be of service to the growth of the trees, by equally attracting the juices of the earth. I should lop off the aspiring tops of my olive; it will spread more beautifully into a round form, and will produce fruit on more branches. A horse with slender flanks is considered handsomer than one not framed in that manner, and the same quality also shows that he excels in swiftness. An athlete whose arms from exercise show a full spring and play of the muscles, is a beautiful sight, and he, likewise, is best fitted as a combatant. Thus the true species is never without its utility, as even a meager judgment easily may discern.

DEVELOPING VARIETY OF STYLE

But it will be of more importance to observe that this decent attire ought to be varied according to the nature of the subject. To begin with our first division, the same style will not suit equally demonstrative, deliberative, and judicial causes. The first, calculated for ostentation, aims at nothing but the pleasure of the auditory. It, therefore, displays all the riches of art, and exposes to full view all the pomp of eloquence; not acting by stratagem, nor striving for victory, but making praise and glory its sole and ultimate end. Whatever may be pleasing in the thought, beautiful in the expression, agreeable in the turn, magnificent in the metaphor, elaborate in the composition, the orator will lay open for inspection and, if it were possible, for handling, as a merchant exposes his wares; for here the success wholly regards him and not the cause.

But when the serious part of a trial is on hand, and the contest is truly in earnest, care of reputation ought to be the orator's last concern. For this reason, when everything in a way is at stake, no one ought to be solicitous about words. I do not say that no ornaments ought to have place in them, but that they should be more modest and severe, less apparent, and above all suited to the subject. For in deliberations the senate require something more elevated; the assemblies of the people, something more spirited; and at the bar, public and capital causes, something more accurate. But a private deliberation, and causes of trivial consequence, as the stating of accounts and the like, need little beyond the plain and easy manner of common discourse. Would it not be quite shameful to demand in elaborate periods the payment of money lent, or appeal to the emotions in speaking of the repairs of a gutter or sink?

THE CHOICE OF WORDS

As the ornament, as well as perspicuity, of speech consists either in single words or in many together, we shall consider what they require separately and what in conjunction. Tho there is good reason for saying that perspicuity is best suited by proper words, and ornament by metaphorical, yet we should always know that an impropriety is never ornamental. But as many words very often signify the same thing, and therefore are called synonymous, some of these must be more sublime, more bright, more agreeable, and sweeter and fuller in pronunciation than others. As the more clear-sounding letters communicate the same quality to the syllables they compose, so the words composed of these syllables become more sonorous, and the greater the force or sound of the syllables is, the more they fill or charm the ear. What the junction of syllables makes, the copulation of words makes also, a word sounding well with one, which sound badly with another.

There is a great diversity in the use of words. Harsh words best express things of an atrocious nature. In general, the best of simple words are believed to be such as sound loudest in exclamation, or sweetest in a pleasing strain. Modest words will ever be preferred to those that must offend a chaste ear, and no polite discourse ever makes allowance for a filthy or sordid expression. Magnificent, noble, and sublime words are to be estimated by their congruity with the subject; for what is magnificent in one place, swells into bombast in another; and what is low in a grand matter, may be proper in a humble situation. As in a splendid style a low word must be very much out of place and, as it were, a blemish to it, so a sublime and pompous expression is unsuited to a subject that is plain and familiar, and therefore must be reputed corrupt, because it raises that which ought to find favor through its native simplicity.

THE MANNER OF DELIVERY

I shall pass now to the construction of words, observing that their ornamental use may be considered from two points of view; first, as it regards the elocution we conceive in our minds; second, the manner of expressing it. It is of particular consequence that we should be clear as to what ought to be amplified or diminished; whether we are to speak with heat or moderation; in a florid or austere style; in a copious or concise manner; in words of bitter invective, or in those showing placid and gentle disposition; with magnificence or plainness; gravity or politeness. Besides which it is equally important to know what metaphors, what figures, what thoughts, what manner, what disposition, are best suited for effecting our purpose.

FAULTS OF EXPRESSION TO AVOID

In speaking of the ornaments of a discourse, it may not be amiss to touch first upon qualities contrary to them, because the principal perfection consists in being free from faults. We, therefore, must not expect ornament that is not probable, in a discourse. Cicero calls that kind of ornament probable which is not more nor less than it ought to be. Not that it should not appear neat and polished, for this is a part of ornament, but because too much in anything is always a fault. He would have authority and weight in words, and thoughts that are sensible, or conformable to the opinions and manners of men. These inviolably retained and adhered to, he makes ample allowance for whatever else may contribute to illustrate a discourse. And thus it is that metaphors, superlatives, epithets, compound, and synonymous words, if they seem to express the action and fully represent things, seldom fail to please.

We should avoid the fault which makes a sentence appear not full enough, on account of something defective, tho this is rather a vice of obscurity than want of ornament in speech. But when it is done for some particular reason, then it becomes a figure of speech. We should likewise be aware of tautology, which is a repetition of the same word or thought, or the use of many similar words or thoughts. Tho this does not seem to have been much guarded against by some authors of great note, it is, notwithstanding, a fault, and Cicero himself often falls into it.

Similarity of expression is a still greater vice, because the mind is wearied by lack of the graces of variety, and the discourse being all of one color, shows a great deficiency in the art of oratory. It, besides, creates loathing, and at length becomes insupportable, both to the mind and ear, through the tedious repetition of the same cold thoughts, figures, and periods.

There is another fault, that of being over-nice, which is caused by extreme anxiety to be exact, but which is as far distant from exactness as superstition is from true religion. In short, every word that contributes neither to perspicuity nor ornament, may be called vicious.

A perverse affectation is faulty in all respects. All bombast, and flimsiness, and studied sweetness, and redundancies, and far-fetched thoughts, and witticisms, fall under the same denomination. Thus whatever stretches beyond the bounds of perfection, may be called affectation, and this happens as often as the genius is lacking in judgment, and suffers itself to be deceived by an appearance of good. It is the worst of vices in matters of eloquence, for even when others are avoided, this is sought after, and its whole trespass is against elocution. There are vices incident to things, which come from being devoid of sense, or from being common, or contrary, or unnecessary, and a corrupt style consists principally in impropriety of words, in their redundancy, in their obscure import, in a weak composition, and in a puerile hunting after synonymous or equivocal words. But every perverse affectation is false in consequence of its idea, tho not everything that is false is an affectation, the latter saying a thing otherwise than as nature will have it, and than it ought to be, and than is sufficient.

USE OF VIVID DESCRIPTION

There can not be a greater perfection than to express the things we speak of in such lively colors as to make them seem really to take place in our presence. Our words are lacking in full effect, they assume not that absolute empire they ought to have, when they strike only the ear, and when the judge who is to take cognizance of the matter is not sensible of its being emphatically exprest.

One manner of representation consists in making out of an assemblage of circumstances the image we endeavor to exhibit. An example of this we have in Cicero's description of a riotous banquet; he being the only one who can furnish us with examples of all kinds of ornaments: "I seemed to myself to see some coming in, others going out; some tottering with drunkenness, others yawning from yesterday's carousing. In the midst of these was Gallius, bedaubed with essences, and crowned with flowers. The floor of their apartment was all in a muck of dirt, streaming with wine, and strewed all about with chaplets of faded flowers, and fish-bones." Who could have seen more had he been present?

In this manner pity grows upon us from hearing of the sacking of a town. Undoubtedly he who acquaints us of such an event, comprehends all the incidents of so great a calamity, yet this cursory piece of intelligence makes but a languid impression upon the mind. But if you enter into descriptive pictures of all that was included in one word, as it were, flames will appear spreading through houses and temples; the crash of falling houses will be heard; and one confused noise formed out of all together. Some will be seen striving to escape the danger, but know not where to direct their flight; others embracing for the last time their parents and relations; here the dismal shrieks of women and piercing cries of children fill one with pity; there the sighs and groans of old men, lamenting their unhappy fate for having lived so long as to be witnesses of their country's desolation. A further addition to these scenes of woe is the plunder of all things, sacred as well as profane; the avidity of the soldier prowling after and carrying away his prey; the wretched citizens dragged away in chains before their haughty conquerors; mothers struggling to keep with them their children; and slaughter still exercising its cruelties wherever there is the least expectation of booty. Tho all these details are comprehended in the idea of the sacking of a town, yet it is saying less to state merely that the town was sacked than to describe its destruction in this circumstantial manner.

Such circumstances may be made to appear vivid if they retain a likeness to truth. They may not have happened in reality, yet, as they are possible, the descriptive evidence is not objectionable. The same evidence will arise also from accidents, as in the following examples:

> ... me horror chills,
> Shudd'ring, and fear congeals my curdling blood.
>
> TRAPP.

> ... to their bosoms press'd,
> The frighted mothers clasp'd their crying babes.
>
> TRAPP.

This perfection, the greatest, in my opinion, a discourse can have, is very easily acquired by only considering and following nature. For eloquence is a picture of the happenings of human life, every one applying to himself what he hears, by making the case in some measure his own, and the mind receives very willingly that with which it has become familiar.

To throw light, also, upon things, similes have been invented, some of which by way of proof are inserted among arguments, and others are calculated for expressing the images of things, the point we are here explaining.

> ... Thence like wolves
> Prowling in gloomy shade, which hunger blind
> Urges along, while their forsaken whelps
> Expect them with dry jaws.
>
> TRAPP.

> ... Thence with all his body's force
> Flings himself headlong from the steepy height
> Down to the ocean: like the bird that flies
> Low, skimming o'er the surface, near the sea,
> Around the shores, around the fishy rocks.
>
> TRAPP.

HOW TO EMPLOY SIMILES AND METAPHORS

We must be exceedingly cautious in regard to similitudes, that we do not use such as are either obscure or unknown. For that which is assumed for the sake of illustrating another thing, ought indeed to be clearer than that which it so illustrates.

In speaking of arguments I mentioned a kind of similitude which, as an ornament to a discourse, contributes to make it sublime, florid, pleasing, and admirable. For the more far-fetched a similitude is, the more new and unexpected it will appear. Some may be thought commonplace, yet will avail much for enforcing belief; as, "As a piece of ground becomes better and more fertile by cultivation, so does the mind by good institutions." "As physicians prescribe the amputation of a limb that manifestly tends to mortification, so would it be necessary to cut off all bad citizens, tho even allied to us in blood." Here is something more sublime: "Rocks and solitudes echo back the melody, and the fiercest beasts are often made more gentle, being astonished by the harmony of music." But this kind of similitude is often abused by the too great liberties our declaimers give themselves; for they use such as are false, and they do not make a just application of them to the subjects to which they would compare them.

In every comparison the similitude either goes before, and the thing follows; or the thing goes before, and the similitude follows. But the similitude sometimes is free and separate: sometimes, which is best, it is connected with the thing of which it is the image, this connection being made to aid and correspond mutually on both sides. Cicero says in his oration for Murena: "They who have not a genius for playing on the lyre, may become expert at playing on the flute (a proverbial saying among the Greeks to specify the man who can not make himself master of the superior sciences): so among us they who can not become orators, turn to the study of the law." In another passage of the same oration, the connected comparison is conceived in a sort of poetical spirit. "As storms are often raised by the influence of some constellation, and often suddenly and from some hidden cause which can not be accounted for, so the stormy agitations we sometimes behold in the assemblies of the people are often occasioned by a malign influence easily discoverable by all; and often their cause is so obscure as to seem merely the effect of chance." There are other similes, which are very short, as this, "Strolling and wandering through forests like beasts." And that of Cicero against Clodius, "From which judgment we have seen him escape naked, like a man from his house on fire." Such similes constantly occur in common discourse.

Of a similar kind is an ornament which not only represents things, but does so in a lively and concise manner. Undoubtedly a conciseness in which nothing is lacking, is deservedly praised; that which says precisely only what is necessary, is less estimable; but that which expresses much in a few words is of all the most beautiful.

Eloquence does not think it enough to show of what it speaks, in a clear and evident manner; it uses, besides, a variety of other expedients for embellishing a discourse. Thus it is that a simple and unaffected style is not without beauty, but it is a beauty entirely pure and natural, such as is admired in women. Beauty is also annexed to propriety and justness of expression, and this beauty is the more elegant as it shows but little care. There is an abundance that is rich, an abundance that smiles amidst the gaiety of flowers, and there is more than one sort of power, for whatever is complete in its kind can not be destitute of its proper strength and efficacy.

COMPOSITION AND STYLE

I well know that there are some who will not sanction any care in composition, contending that our words as they flow by chance, however uncouth they may sound, are not only more natural, but likewise more manly. If what first sprang from nature, indebted in nowise to care and industry, be only what they deem natural, I admit that the art of oratory in this respect has no pretensions to that quality. For it is certain that the first men did not speak according to the exactness of the rules of composition; neither were they acquainted with the art of preparing by an exordium, informing by a narration, proving by arguments, and moving by passions. They were deficient in all these particulars, and not in composition only; and if they were not allowed to make any alterations for the better, of course they would not have exchanged their cottages for houses, nor their coverings of skins for more decent apparel, nor the mountains and forests in which they ranged for the abode of cities in which they enjoy the comforts of social intercourse. And, indeed, what art do we find coeval with the world, and what is there of which the value is not enhanced by improvement? Why do we restrain the luxuriance of our vines? Why do we dig about them? Why do we grub up the bramble-bushes in our fields? Yet the earth produces them. Why do we tame animals? Yet are they born with intractable dispositions. Rather let us say that that is very natural which nature permits us to meliorate in her handiwork.

THE POWER OF SKILFUL COMPOSITION

How can a jumble of uncouth words be more manly than a manner of expression which is well joined and properly placed? If some authors weaken the subjects of which they treat, by straining them into certain soft and lascivious measures, we must not on that account judge that this is the fault of composition. As the current of rivers is swifter and more impetuous in a free and open channel than amidst an obstruction of rocks breaking and struggling against the flow of their waters, an oration that is properly connected flows with its whole might, and is far preferable to one that is craggy and desultory by reason of frequent interruptions. Why, then, should it be thought that strength and beauty are incompatible, when, on the contrary, nothing has its just value without art, and embellishment always attends on it? Do not we observe the javelin which has been cleverly whirled about, dart through the air with the best effect; and in managing a bow and arrow, is not the beauty of the attitude as much more graceful as the aim is more unerring? In feats of arms, and in all the exercises of the palæstra, is not his attitude best calculated for defense or offense, who uses a certain art in all his motions, and keeps to a certain position of the feet? Composition, therefore, in my opinion, is to thoughts and words what the dexterous management of a bow or string may be for directing the aim of missive weapons; and I may say that the most learned are convinced that it is greatly conducive not only to pleasure, but also to making a good impression on others. First, because it is scarcely possible that anything should affect the heart, which begins by grating on the ear. Secondly, because we are naturally affected by harmony, otherwise the sounds of musical instruments, tho they express no words, would not excite in us so great a variety of pleasing emotions. In sacred canticles, some airs are for elating the heart into raptures, others to restore the mind to its former tranquillity. The sound of a trumpet is not the same when it is the signal for a general engagement, and when on defeat it implores the conqueror's mercy; neither is it the same when an army marches up to give battle, and when it is intent on retreating. It was a common practise with the Pythagoric philosophers, on arising in the morning, to awake their minds by an air on the lyre, in order to make them more alert for action; and they had recourse to the same musical entertainment for disposing them to sleep, believing it to be a means for allaying all tumultuous thoughts which might in any way have ruffled them in the course of the day.

If, then, so great a power lies in musical strains and modulations, what must it be with eloquence, the music of which is a speaking harmony? As much, indeed, as it is essential for a thought to be exprest in suitable words, it is equally necessary for the same words to be disposed in proper order by composition, that they may flow and end harmoniously. Some things of little consequence in their import, and requiring but a moderate degree of elocution, are commendable only by this perfection; and there are others which appear exprest with so much force, beauty, and sweetness, that if the order in which they stand should be changed or disturbed, all force, beauty, and sweetness would vanish from them.

THE ESSENTIALS OF GOOD COMPOSITION

There are three things necessary in every kind of composition, and these are order, correction, and number.

1. Order

We shall speak first of order, which applies to words considered separately or joined together. In regard to the former, care must be taken that there be no decrease by adding a weaker word to a stronger, as accusing one of sacrilege, and giving him afterward the name of thief; or adding the character of wanton fellow to that of a highwayman. The sense ought to increase and rise, which Cicero observes admirably where he says: "And thou, with that voice, those lungs, and that gladiator-like vigor of thy whole body." Here each succeeding thing is stronger than the one before; but if he had begun with the whole body, he could not with propriety have descended to the voice and lungs. There is another natural order in saying men and women, day and night, east and west.

Words in prose not being measured, as are the feet which compose verse, they are, therefore, transferred from place to place, that they may be joined where they best fit, as in a building where the irregularity, however great, of rough stones is both suitable and proper. The happiest composition language can have, however, is to keep to a natural order, just connection, and a regularly flowing cadence.

Sometimes there is something very striking about a word. Placed in the middle of a sentence, it might pass unnoticed, or be obscured by the other words that lie about it, but when placed at the end the auditor can not help noting it and retaining it in his mind.

2. Connection

Juncture follows, which is equally requisite in words, articles, members, and periods, all these having their beauty and faults, in consequence of their manner of connection. It may be a general observation that in the placing of syllables, their sound will be harsher as they are pronounced with a like or different gaping of the mouth. This, however, is not to be dreaded as a signal fault, and I know not which is worse here, inattention or too great care. Too scrupulous fear must damp the heat and retard the impetuosity of speaking, while at the same time it prevents the mind from attending to thoughts which are of greater moment. As, therefore, it is carelessness to yield to these faults, so it is meanness to be too much afraid of them.

3. Number

Numbers are nowhere so much lacking, nor so remarkable, as at the end of periods; first, because every sense has its bounds, and takes up a natural space, by which it is divided from the beginning of what follows: next, because the hearers following the flow of words, and drawn, as it were, down the current of the oration, are then more competent judges, when that impetuosity ceases and gives time for reflection. There should not, therefore, be anything harsh nor abrupt in that ending, which seems calculated for the respite and recreation of the mind and ear. This, too, is the resting-place of the oration, this the auditor expects, and here burst forth all his effusions of praise.

THE COMPOSITION OF PERIODS

The beginning of periods demands as much care as the closing of them, for here, also, the auditor is attentive. But it is easier to observe numbers in the beginning of periods, as they are not depending on, nor connected with, what went before. But the ending of periods, however graceful it may be in composition and numbers, will lose all its charm if we proceed to it by a harsh and precipitate beginning.

As to the composition of the middle parts of a period, care must be taken not only of their connection with each other, but also that they may not seem slow, nor long, nor, what is now a great vice, jump and start from being made up of many short syllables, and producing the same effect on the ear as the sounds from a child's rattle. For as the ordering of the beginning and ending is of much importance, as often as the sense begins or ends; so in the middle, too, there is a sort of stress which slightly insists; as the feet of people running, which, tho they make no stop, yet leave a track. It is not only necessary to begin and end well the several members and articles, but the intermediate space, tho continued without respiration, ought also to retain a sort of composition, by reason of the insensible pauses that serve as so many degrees for pronunciation.

Cicero gives many names to the period, calling it a winding about, a circuit, a comprehension, continuation, and circumscription. It is of two kinds; the one simple when a single thought is drawn out into a considerable number of words; the other compound, consisting of members and articles which include several thoughts.

Wherever the orator has occasion to conduct himself severely, to press home, to act boldly and resolutely, he should speak by members and articles. This manner has vast power and efficacy in an oration. The composition is to adapt itself to the nature of things, therefore, even rough things being conceived in rough sounds and numbers, that the hearer may be made to enter into all the passions of the speaker. It would be advisable, for the most part, to make the narration in members; or if periods are used, they ought to be more loose and less elaborate than elsewhere. But I except such narrations as are calculated more for ornament than for giving information.

THE USE OF PERIODS

The period is proper for the exordiums of greater causes, where the matter requires solicitude, commendation, pity. Also in common places and in every sort of amplification; but if you accuse, it ought to be close and compact; if you praise, it should be full, round, and flowing. It is likewise of good service in perorations, and may be used without restriction wherever the composition requires to be set off in a somewhat grand and noble manner, and when the judge not only has a thorough knowledge of the matter before him, but is also captivated with the beauty of the discourse and, trusting to the orator, allows himself to be led away by the sense of pleasure.

History does not so much stand in need of a periodical flow of words, as it likes to move around in a sort of perpetual circle, for all its members are connected with each other, by its slipping and gliding along from one subject to the next, just as men, strengthening their pace, hold and are held, by grasping each other by the hand. Whatever belongs to the demonstrative kind has freer and more flowing numbers. The judicial and deliberative, being varied in their matter, occasionally require a different form of composition.

FITTING EXPRESSION TO THOUGHT

Who doubts that some things are to be exprest in a gentle way, others with more heat, others sublimely, others contentiously, and others gravely? Feet composed of long syllables best suit grave, sublime, and ornamental subjects. The grave will take up a longer space in the pronunciation, and the sublime and ornamental will demand a clear and sonorous expression. Feet of short syllables are more agreeable in arguments, division, raillery, and whatever partakes of the nature of ordinary conversation.

The composition of the exordium will differ, therefore, as the subject may require. For the mind of the judge is not always the same, so that, according to the time and circumstances, we must declare our mournful plight, appear modest, tart, grave, insinuating; move to mercy and exhort to diligence. As the nature of these is different, so their composition must be conducted in a different way.

Let it be in some measure a general observation that the composition ought to be modeled on the manner of pronunciation. In exordiums are we not most commonly modest, except when in a cause of accusation we strive to irritate the minds of the judges? Are we not copious and explicit in narration; in arguments animated and lively, even showing animation in our actions; in common places and descriptions, exuberant and lavish of ornaments; and in perorations, for the most part weighed down by distress? Of the variety which ought to be in a discourse, we may find another parallel instance in the motions of the body. With all of them, do not the circumstances regulate their respective degrees of slowness and celerity? And for dancing as well as singing, does not music use numbers of which the beating of the time makes us sensible? As our voice and action are indeed expressive of our inner feelings in regard to the nature of the things of which we speak, need we, then, be surprized if a like conformity ought to be found in the feet that enter into the composition of a piece of eloquence? Ought not sublime matters be made to walk in majestic solemnity, the mild to keep in a gentle pace, the brisk and lively to bound with rapidity, and the nice and delicate to flow smoothly?

FAULTS IN COMPOSITION

If faults in composition be unavoidable, I should rather give preference to that which is harsh and rough than to that which is nerveless and weak, the results of an affected style that many now study, and which constantly corrupts, more and more, by a wantonness in numbers more becoming a dance than the majesty of eloquence. But I can not say that any composition is good, however perfect otherwise, which constantly presents the same form, and continually falls into the same feet. A constant observing of similar measures and cadences, is a kind of versification, and all prose in which this fault is discoverable, can have no allowance made for it, by reason of its manifest affectation (the very suspicion of which ought to be avoided), and its uniformity, which, of course, must fatigue and disgust the mind. This vice may have some engaging charms at first sight, but the greater its sweets are, the shorter will be their continuance; and the orator once detected of any anxious concern in this respect, will instantly lose all belief that has been placed in him, and vainly will he strive to make on others' minds the impressions he expected to make; for how is it to be expected that a judge will believe a man, or permit himself to feel grief or anger on account of one whom he observes to have attended to nothing more than the display of such trifles? Some of the connections of smooth composition ought, therefore, to be designedly broken, and it is no small labor to make them appear not labored.

Let us not be such slaves to the placing of words as to study transpositions longer than necessary, lest what we do in order to please, may displease by being affected. Neither let a fondness for making the composition flow with smoothness, prevail on us to set aside a word otherwise proper and becoming; as no word, in reality, can prove disagreeable enough to be wholly excluded, unless it be that in the avoiding of such words we consult mere beauty of expression rather than the good of composition.

To conclude, composition ought to be graceful, agreeable, varied. Its parts are three: order, connection, number. Its art consists in adding, retrenching, changing. Its qualities are according to the nature of the things discust. The care in composition ought to be great, but not to take the place of care in thinking and speaking. What deserves to be particularly attended to is the concealing of the care of composition, that the numbers may seem to flow of their own accord, and not with the least constraint or affectation.

COPIOUSNESS OF WORDS

Eloquence will never be solid and robust, unless it collects strength and consistence from much writing and composing; and without examples from reading, that labor will go astray for lack of a guide; and tho it be known how everything ought to be said, yet the orator who is not possest of a talent for speaking, always ready to exert himself on occasion, will be like a man watching over a hidden treasure.

Our orator, who we suppose is familiar with the way of inventing and disposing things, of making a choice of words, and placing them in proper order, requires nothing further than the knowledge of the means whereby in the easiest and best manner he may execute what he has learned. It can not, then, be doubted that he must acquire a certain stock of wealth in order to have it ready for use when needed, and this stock of wealth consists of a plentiful supply of things and words.

THE RIGHT WORD IN THE RIGHT PLACE

Things are peculiar to each cause, or common to few; but a provision of words must be made indiscriminately for all subjects. If each word were precisely significant of each thing, our perplexity would be less, as then words would immediately present themselves with things, but some being more proper than others, or more ornamental, or more emphatic, or more harmonious, all ought not only to be known but to be kept ready and in sight, as it were, that when they present themselves for the orator's selection, he easily may make a choice of the best.

I know that some make a practise of classing together all synonymous words and committing them to memory, so that out of so many at least one may more easily come to mind; and when they have used a word, and shortly after need it again, to avoid repetition they take another of the same significance. This is of little or no use, for it is only a crowd that is mustered together, out of which the first at hand is taken indifferently, whereas the copiousness of language of which I speak is to be the result of acquisition of judgment in the use of words, with the view of attaining the true expressive force of eloquence, and not empty volubility of speech. This can be affected only by hearing and reading the best things; and it is only by giving it our attention that we shall know not only the appellations of things, but what is fittest for every place.

THE VALUE OF HEARING SPEAKERS

With some eloquent compositions we may derive more profit by reading them, but with some others, more by hearing them pronounced. The speaker keeps awake all our senses, and inspires us by the fire that animates him. We are struck, not by the image and exterior of things, but by the things themselves. All is life and motion, and with solicitude for his success, we favorably receive all he says, its appeal to us lying in the charm of novelty. Together with the orator, we find ourselves deeply interested in the issue of the trial and the safety of the parties whose defense he has undertaken. Besides these we find that other things affect us: a fine voice, a graceful action corresponding with what is said, and a manner of pronunciation, which perhaps is the most powerful ornament of eloquence; in short, everything conducted and managed in the way that is most fitting.

THE ADVANTAGES OF READING

In reading, our judgment goes upon surer ground, because often our good wishes for the speaker, or the applause bestowed on him, surprizes us into approbation. We are ashamed to differ in opinion from others, and by a sort of secret bashfulness are kept from believing ourselves more intelligent than they are; tho indeed we are aware, at the same time, that the taste of the greater number is vicious, and that sycophants, even persons hired to applaud, praise things which can not please us; as, on the other hand, it also happens that a bad taste can have no relish for the best things. Reading is attended, besides, with the advantage of being free, and not escaping us by the rapidity which accompanies action; and we may go over the same things often, should we doubt their accuracy, or wish to fix them in our memories. Repeating and reviewing will, therefore, be highly necessary; for as meats are chewed before they descend into the stomach, in order to facilitate their digestion, so reading is fittest for being laid up in the memory, that it may be an object of imitation when it is no longer in a crude state but has been softened and elaborated by long meditation.

HOW TO READ MOST PROFITABLY

None, however, but the best authors, and such as we are least liable to be deceived in, demand this care, which should be diligent and extended even almost to the point of taking the pains to transcribe them. Nor ought judgment to be passed on the whole from examining a part, but after the book has been fully perused, it should have a second reading; especially should this be done with an oration, the perfections of which are often designedly kept concealed. The orator, indeed, often prepares, dissembles, lies in wait, and says things in the first part of the pleading which he avails himself of in the last part. They may, therefore, be less pleasing in their place, while we still remain ignorant of the purpose for their being said. For this reason, after a due consideration of particulars, it would not be amiss to re-read the whole.

WHAT TO READ

Theophrastus says that the reading of poetry is of vast service to the orator. Many, and with good reason, are of the same opinion, as from the poets may be derived sprightliness in thought, sublimity in expression, force and variety in sentiment, propriety and decorum in character, together with that diversion for cheering and freshening minds which have been for any time harassed by the drudgery of the bar.

Let it be remembered, however, that poets are not in all things to be imitated by the orator, neither in the liberty of words, nor license of figures. The whole of that study is calculated for ostentation. Its sole aim is pleasure, and it invariably pursues it, by fictions of not only what is false, but of some things that are incredible. It is sure, also, of meeting with partizans to espouse its cause, because, since it is bound down to a certain necessity of feet it can not always use proper words, and being driven out of the straight road, must turn into byways of speaking, and be compelled to change some words, and to lengthen, shorten, transpose and divide them. As for orators, they must stand their ground completely armed in the order of battle, and having to fight for matters of the highest consequence, must think of nothing but gaining the victory.

Still would I not have their armor appear squalid and covered with rust, but retain rather a brightness that dismays, such as of polished steel, striking both the mind and eyes with awe, and not the splendor of gold and silver, a weak safeguard, indeed, and rather dangerous to the bearer.

History, likewise, by its mild and grateful sap may afford kind nutriment to an oratorical composition. Yet the orator should so read history as to be convinced that most of its perfections ought to be avoided by him. It nearly borders upon poetry, and may be held as a poem, unrestrained by the laws of verse. Its object is to narrate, and not to prove, and its whole business neither intends action nor contention, but to transmit facts to posterity, and enhance the reputation of its author.

In the reading of history there is another benefit, and indeed the greatest, but one not relative to the present subject. This proceeds from the knowledge of things and examples, which the orator ought to be well versed in, so that not all his testimonies may be from the parties, but many of them may be taken from antiquity, with which, through history, he will be well acquainted; these testimonies being the more powerful, as they are exempt from suspicion of prejudice and partiality.

I shall venture to say that there are few which have stood the test of time, that may not be read with some profit by the judicious. Cicero himself confesses that he received great help from old authors, who were, indeed, very ingenious but were deficient in art. Before I speak of the respective merit of authors, I must make, in a few words, some general reflections on the diversity of taste in regard to matters of eloquence. Some think that the ancients deserve to be read, believing that they alone have distinguished themselves by natural eloquence and that strength of language so becoming men. Others are captivated with the flowery profusion of the orators of the present age, with their delicate turns, and with all the blandishments they skilfully invent to charm the ears of an ignorant multitude. Some choose to follow the plain and direct way of speaking. Others take to be sound and truly Attic whatever is close, neat, and departs but little from ordinary conversation. Some are delighted with a more elevated, more impetuous, and more fiery force of genius. Others, and not a few, like a smooth, elegant, and polite manner. I shall speak of this difference in taste more fully when I come to examine the style which may seem most proper for the orator.

QUALITIES OF CLASSIC WRITERS

Homer

We may begin properly with Homer.

He it is who gave birth to, and set the example for all parts of eloquence, in the same way, as he himself says, as the course of rivers and springs of fountains owe their origin to the ocean. No one, in great subjects, has excelled him in elevation; nor in small subjects, in propriety. He is florid and close, grave and agreeable, admirable for his concise as well as for his copious manner, and is not only eminent for poetical, but likewise oratorical, abilities.

Æschylus

Æschylus is the one who gave birth to tragedy. He is sublime, and grave, and often pompous to a fault. But his plots are mostly ill-contrived and as ill-conducted. For which reason the Athenians permitted the poets who came after him to correct his pieces and fit them for the stage, and in this way many of these poets received the honor of being crowned.

Sophocles and Euripides

Sophocles and Euripides brought tragedy to greater perfection; but the difference in their manner has occasioned dispute among the learned as to their relative poetic merits. For my part, I shall leave the matter undecided, as having nothing to do with my present purpose. It must be confest, nevertheless, that the study of Euripedes will be of much greater value to those who are preparing themselves for the bar; for besides the fact that his style comes nearer the oratorical style, he likewise abounds in fine thoughts, and in philosophic maxims is almost on an equality with philosophers, and in his dialog may be compared with the best speakers at the bar. He is wonderful, again, for his masterly strokes in moving the passions, and more especially in exciting sympathy.

Thucydides and Herodotus

There have been many famous writers of history, but all agree in giving the preference to two, whose perfections, tho different, have received an almost equal degree of praise. Thucydides is close, concise, and ever pressing on. Herodotus is sweet, natural, and copious. One is remarkable for his animated expression of the more impetuous passions, the other for gentle persuasion in the milder: the former succeeds in harangues and has more force; the other surpasses in speeches of familiar intercourse, and gives more pleasure.

Demosthenes

A numerous band of orators follows, for Athens produced ten of them, contemporary with one another. Demosthenes was by far the chief of them, and in a manner held to be the only model for eloquence; so great is his force; so closely together are all things interwoven in his discourse, and attended with a certain self-command; so great is his accuracy, he never adopting any idle expression; and so just his precision that nothing lacking, nothing redundant, can be found in him. Æschines is more full, more diffusive, and appears the more grand, as he has more breadth. He has more flesh, but not so many sinews.

Lysias and Isocrates

Lysias, older than these, is subtle and elegant, and if it is enough for the orator to instruct, none could be found more perfect than he is. There is nothing idle, nothing far-fetched in him; yet is he more like a clear brook than a great river. Isocrates, in a different kind of eloquence, is fine and polished, and better adapted for engaging in a mock than a real battle. He was attentive to all the beauties of discourse, and had his reasons for it, having intended his eloquence for schools and not for contentions at the bar. His invention was easy, he was very fond of graces and embellishments, and so nice was he in his composition that his extreme care is not without reprehension.

Plato

Among philosophers, by whom Cicero confesses he has been furnished with many resourceful aids to eloquence, who doubts that Plato is the chief, whether we consider the acuteness of his dissertations, or his divine Homerical faculty of elocution? He soars high above prose, and even common poetry, which is poetry only because comprised in a certain number of feet; and he seems to me not so much endowed with the wit of a man, as inspired by a sort of Delphic oracle.

Xenophon

What shall I say of Xenophon's unaffected agreeableness, so unattainable by any imitation that the Graces themselves seem to have composed his language? The testimony of the ancient comedy concerning Pericles, is very justly applicable to him, "That the Goddess of Persuasion had seated herself on his lips."

Aristotle and Theophrastus

And what shall I say of the elegance of the other disciples of Socrates? What of Aristotle? I am at a loss to know what most to admire in him, his vast and profound erudition, or the great number of his writings, or his pleasing style and manner, or the inventions and penetration of his wit, or the variety of his works. And as to Theophrastus, his elocution has something so noble and so divine that it may be said that from these qualities came his name.

Vergil

In regard to our Roman authors, we can not more happily begin than with Vergil, who of all their poets and ours in the epic style, is without any doubt the one who comes nearest to Homer. Tho obliged to give way to Homer's heavenly and immortal genius, yet in Vergil are to be found a greater exactness and care, it being incumbent on him to take more pains; so that what we lose on the side of eminence of qualities, we perhaps gain on that of justness and equability.

Cicero

I proceed to our orators, who likewise may put Roman eloquence upon a par with the Grecian. Cicero I would strenuously oppose against any of them, tho conscious of the quarrel I should bring upon myself by comparing him with Demosthenes in a time so critical as this; especially as my subject does not oblige me to it, neither is it of any consequence, when it is my real opinion that Demosthenes ought to be particularly read, or, rather, committed to memory.

I must say, notwithstanding, that I judge them to be alike in most of the great qualities they possess; alike in design, disposition, manner of dividing, of preparing minds, of proving, in short in everything belonging to invention. In elocution there is some difference. The one is more compact, the other more copious; the one closes in with his opponent, the other allows him more ground to fight in; the one is always subtle and keen in argument, the other is perhaps less so, but often has more weight; from the one nothing can be retrenched, neither can anything be added to the other; the one has more study, the other more nature.

Still ought we to yield, if for no other reason than because Demosthenes lived before Cicero, and because the Roman orator, however great, is indebted for a large part of his merit to the Athenian. For it seems to me that Cicero, having bent all his thoughts on the Greeks, toward forming himself on their model, had at length made constituents of his character the force of Demosthenes, the abundance of Plato, and the sweetness of Isocrates. Nor did he only, by his application, extract what was best in these great originals, but by the happy fruitfulness of his immortal genius he himself produced the greater part, or rather all, of these same perfections. And to make use of an expression of Pindar, he does not collect the water from rains to remedy a natural dryness, but flows continually, himself, from a source of living waters, and seems to have existed by a peculiar gift of Providence, that in him eloquence might make trial of her whole strength and her most powerful exertions.

For who can instruct with more exactness, and move with more vehemence? What orator ever possest so pleasing a manner that the very things he forcibly wrests from you, you fancy you grant him; and when by his violence he carries away the judge, yet does the judge seem to himself to obey his own volition, and not to be swept away by that of another? Besides, in all he says there is so much authority and weight that you are ashamed to differ from him in opinion; and it is not the zeal of an advocate you find in him, but rather the faith and sincerity of a witness or judge. And what, at the same time, is more admirable, all these qualities, any one of which could not be attained by another without infinite pains, seem to be his naturally; so that his discourses, the most charming, the most harmonious, which possibly can be heard, retain, notwithstanding, so great an air of happy ease that they seem to have cost him nothing.

With good reason, therefore, is he said by his contemporaries to reign at the bar, and he has so far gained the good graces of posterity that Cicero is now less the name of a man than the name of eloquence itself. Let us then keep him in view, let him be our model, and let that orator think he has made considerable progress who has once conceived a love and taste for Cicero.

Cæsar

If Cæsar had made the bar his principal occupation, no other of our orators could better have disputed the prize of eloquence with Cicero. So great is his force, so sharp his wit, so active his fire, that it plainly appears he spoke with as much spirit as he fought. A wonderful elegance and purity of language, which he made his particular study, were a further embellishment of all these talents for eloquence.

Philosophers

It remains only to speak of those who have written on subjects of philosophy. Hitherto we have had but few of this kind. Cicero, as in all other respects, so also in this, was a worthy rival of Plato. Brutus has written some excellent treatises, the merit of which is far superior to that of his orations. He supports admirably well the weight of his matter, and seems to feel what he says. Cornelius Celsus, in the manner of the Skeptics, has written a good many tracts, which are not without elegance and perspicuity. Plancus, among the Stoics, may be read with profit, for the sake of becoming acquainted with the things he discusses. Catius, an Epicurean, has some levity in his way, but in the main is not an unpleasing author.

Seneca

I have designedly omitted speaking hitherto of Seneca,—who was proficient in all kinds of eloquence,—on account of the false opinion people entertained that I not only condemned his writings, but also personally hated him. I drew this aspersion upon myself by my endeavor to bring over eloquence to a more austere taste, which had been corrupted and enervated by very many softnesses and delicacies. Then Seneca was almost the only author young people read with pleasure. I did not strive to exclude him absolutely, but could not bear that he should be preferred to others much better, whom he took all possible pains to cry down, because he was conscious that he had taken to a different manner from their way of writing, and he could not otherwise expect to please people who had a taste for these others. It was Seneca's lot, however, to be more loved than imitated, and his partizans run as wide from him as he himself had fallen from the ancients. Yet it were to be wished that they had proved themselves like, or had come near, him. But they were fond of nothing in him but his faults, and every one strove to copy them if he could. Then priding themselves on speaking like Seneca, of course they could not avoid bringing him into disgrace.

His perfections, however, were many and great. His wit was easy and fruitful, his erudition considerable, his knowledge extensive—in which last point he sometimes was led into mistakes, probably by those whom he had charged to make researches for him. There is hardly a branch of study on which he has not written something; for we have his orations, his poems, epistles, and dialogs. In philosophic matters he was not so accurate, but was admirable for his invectives against vice.

He has many bright thoughts, and many things are well worth reading in him for improvement of the moral character; but his elocution is, for the most part, corrupt, and the more dangerous because its vices are of a sweet and alluring nature. One could wish he had written with his own genius and another's judgment. For if he had rejected some things, if he had less studiously affected some engaging beauties, if he had not been overfond of all his productions, if he had not weakened the importance of his matter by frivolous thoughts, he would have been honored by the approbation of the learned rather than by the love of striplings.

However, such as he is, he may be read when the taste is formed and strengthened by a more austere kind of eloquence, if for no other reason than because he can exercise judgment on both sides. For, as I have said, many things in him are worthy of praise, worthy even of admiration if a proper choice had been made, which I wish he had made himself, as indeed that nature is deserving of an inclination to embrace what is better, which has ability to effect anything to which it inclines.

KNOWLEDGE AND SELF-CONFIDENCE

Knowledge of the civil law will, likewise, be necessary for the orator whom we have described, and together with it knowledge of the customs and religion of the commonwealth of which he may take charge, for how shall he be able to give counsel in public and private deliberations if ignorant of the many things which happen together particularly to the establishment of the State? And must he not falsely aver himself to be the patron of the causes he undertakes, if obliged to borrow from another what is of greatest consequence in these causes, in some measure like those who repeat the writings of poets? And how will he accomplish what he has so undertaken if the things which he requires the judge to believe, he shall speak on the faith of another, and if he, the reputed helper of his clients, shall himself stand in need of the help of another?

THOROUGH INFORMATION INDISPENSABLE

But we will suppose him not reduced to this inconvenience, having studied his cause sufficiently at home, and having thoroughly informed himself of all that he has thought proper to lay before the judges: yet what shall become of him when unforeseen questions arise, which often are suddenly started on the back of pleadings? Will he not with great unseemliness look about him? Will he not ask the lower class of advocates how he shall behave? Can he be accurate in comprehending the things then whispered to him, when he is to speak on them instantly? Can he strongly affirm, or speak ingenuously for his clients? Grant that he may in his pleadings, but what shall be his fate in altercation, when he must have his answer ready and he has no time for receiving information? And what if a person learned in the law is not assisting? What if one who knows little of the matter tells him something that is wrong? And this is the greatest mischief in ignorance, to believe such a monitor intelligent.

Now, as we suppose the orator to be a particularly learned and honest man, when he has made sufficient study of that which naturally is best, it will give him little trouble if a lawyer dissents from him in opinion, since even they are admitted to be of different opinions among themselves. But if he desires to know their sentiments on any point of law, he need only read a little, which is the least laborious part of study. If many men who despaired of acquiring the necessary talents for speaking in public, have engaged in the study of law, with how much more ease will the orator effect this, which may be learned by those who from their own confession could not be orators?

M. Cato was as much distinguished by his great eloquence as by his great learning in the law. Scævola and Servius Sulpitius, both eminent lawyers, were also very eloquent. Cicero not only in pleading never appeared at a loss in knowledge of the law, but also began to write some tracts on it. From all these examples it appears that an orator may not less attend to the teaching than the learning of it.

THE MANNER OF THE SPEAKER

I would not have him who is to speak rise unconcerned, show no change of color, and betray no sense of danger,—if they do not happen naturally, they ought at least to be pretended. But this sense should proceed from solicitude for performing well our duty, not from a motive of fear; and we may decently betray emotion, but not faint away. The best remedy, therefore, for bashfulness, is a modest assurance, and however weak the forehead may be, it ought to be lifted up, and well it may by conscious merit.

THE NEED OF GOOD DELIVERY

There are natural aids, as specified before, which are improved by care, and these are the voice, lungs, a good presence, and graceful action, which are advantages sometimes so considerable as to beget a reputation for wit. Our age produced orators more copious than Trachallus, but when he spoke he seemed to surpass them all, so great was the advantage of his stature, the sprightliness of his glance, the majesty of his aspect, the beauty of his action, and a voice, not as Cicero desires it should be, but almost like that of tragedians, and surpassing all the tragedians I ever heard. I well remember that when he once pleaded in the Julian Hall before the first bench of judges, and there also, as usual, the four classes of judges were then sitting, and the whole place rang with noise, he was not only heard distinctly from the four benches, but also was applauded, which was a disparagement to those who spoke after him. But this is the accumulation of what can be wished for, and a happiness hard to be met with, and as it can not fall to every one's lot, let the orator strive at least to make himself heard by those before whom he speaks.

THE TEST OF AN ORATION

Above all, as happens to a great many, let not desire for temporary praise keep our orator from having an eye to the interest of the cause he has undertaken. For as generals in waging wars do not always march their armies over pleasant plains, but often must climb rugged hills, must lay siege to forts and castles raised on steep rocks and mountains, and fortified both by nature and by art: so an orator will be pleased with an opportunity to make great excursions, and when he engages on champion ground, he will display all his forces so as to make an exceedingly fine appearance; but if under the necessity of unraveling the intricacies of some points of law, or placing truth in a clear light from amidst the obscurity thrown around it, he will not then ostentatiously ride about, nor will he use a shower of pointed sentences, as missive weapons; but he will carry on his operations by frustrating his enemy; by mines, by ambuscade, and by stratagem: all of which are not much to be commended while they are being used, but after they have been practised. Whence those men benefit themselves most, who seem least desirous of praise; for when the frivolous parade of eloquence has ceased its bursts of thunder among its own applauders, the more potent applause of true talents will appear in genuine splendor; the judges will not conceal the impressions which have been made on them; the sense of the learned will outweigh the opinion of ignorance: so true it is that it is the winding up of the discourse, and the success attending it, that must prove its true merit.

AVOIDING OSTENTATION

It was customary with the ancients to hide their eloquence; and M. Antonius advises orators so to do, in order that they may be the more believed, and that their stratagems may be less suspected. But the eloquence of those times could well be concealed, not yet having made an accession of so many luminaries as to break out through every intervening obstacle to the transmission of their light. But indeed all art and design should be kept concealed, as most things when once, discovered lose their value. In what I have hitherto spoken of, eloquence loves nothing else so much as privacy. A choice of words, weight of thought, elegance of figures, either do not exist, or they appear. But because they appear, they are not therefore to be displayed with ostentation. Or if one of the two is to be chosen, let the cause rather than the advocate be praised; still the issue will justify him, by his having pleaded excellently a very good cause. It is certain that no one else pleads so ill as he who endeavors to please, while his cause displeases; because the things by which he pleases must necessarily be foreign to his subject.

The orator ought not to be so particular and vain as not to undertake the pleading of the smaller kind of causes, as beneath him, or as if a matter of less consequence should in any respect lessen the reputation he has acquired. Duty indeed is a just motive for his undertaking them, and he should wish that his friends were never engaged in any other kind of suits, which in the main are set off with sufficient eloquence when he has spoken to the purpose.

DO NOT ABUSE YOUR OPPONENT

Some are very liberal in abuse of the advocate of the opposing party, but unless he has brought it upon himself, I think it is acting very ungenerously by him, in consideration of the common duties of the profession. Add to this that these sallies of passion are of no advantage whatever to him who pleads, the opponent having, in his turn, an equal right to abuse; and they may even be harmful to the cause, because the opponent, spurred on to become a real enemy, musters together all the forces of wit to conquer if possible. Above all, that modesty is irrecoverably lost which procures for the orator so much authority and belief, if once departing from the character of a good man, he degenerates into a brawler and barker, conforming himself not to the disposition of the judge, but to the caprice and resentment of the client.

Taking liberties of this kind frequently leads the orator to hazard some rash expressions not less dangerous to the cause than to himself. Pericles was accustomed to wish, with good reason, that no word might ever enter his mind which could give umbrage to the people. But the respect he had for the people ought in my opinion to be had for all, who may have it in their power to do as much hurt; for the words that seemed strong and bold when exprest, are called foolish when they have given offense.

THOROUGH PREPARATION ESSENTIAL

As every orator is remarkable for his manner, the care of one having been imputed to slowness, and the facility of another to rashness, it may not be amiss to point out here a medium. Let him come for pleading prepared with all possible care, as it must argue not only neglect, but also a wicked and treacherous disposition in him, to plead worse than he can in the cause he undertakes, therefore he should not undertake more causes than he is well able to handle.

He should say things, studied and written, in as great a degree as the subject can bear, and, as Demosthenes says, deeply engraven, if it were possible, on his memory, and as perfect as may be. This may be done at the first pleading of a cause, and when in public judgments a cause is adjourned for some time before it comes to a rehearsing. But when a direct reply is to be made, due preparations are impracticable; and even they who are not so ready find what they have written to be rather a prejudice to them if anything unexpectedly is brought forward; for it is with reluctance that they part with what they have prepared, and keeping it in mind during the whole pleading, they are forced to continually wonder if anything can be taken from it to be included in what they are obliged to speak extempore. And tho this may be done, there will still be a lack of connection, and the incoherence will be discoverable from the different coloring and inequality of style. Thus there is neither an uninterrupted fluency in what they say extempore, nor a connection between it and what they recite from memory, for which reason one must be a hindrance to the other, for the written matter will always bring to it the attention of the mind, and scarcely ever follow it. Therefore in these actions, as country-laboring men say, we must stand firmly on our legs. For, as every cause consists of proving and refuting, whatever regards the first may be written, and whatever it is certain the opponent will answer, as sometimes it is certain what he will, may be refuted with equal care and study.

Knowing the cause well is one essential point for being prepared in other respects, and listening attentively to all the opponent states, is another. Still we may previously think of many particular incidents and prepare the mind for all emergencies, this being of special advantage in speaking, the thought being thereby the more easily transmitted and transferred.

But when in answering or otherwise there may be necessity for extempore speaking, the orator will never find himself at a loss and disconcerted, who has been prepared by discipline, and study, and exercise, with the powers of facility, and who, as always under arms and ready for engaging, will no more lack a sufficient flow of speech in the pleading of causes than he does in conversation on daily and domestic occurrences; neither will he ever, for lack of coming duly prepared, decline burdening himself with a cause, if he has time to learn the state of it, for with anything else he always will be well acquainted.

CONCLUSION

The orator having distinguished himself by these perfections of eloquence at the bar, in counsels, in the assemblies of the people, in the senate, and in all the duties of a good citizen, ought to think, likewise, of making an end worthy of an honest man and the sanctity of his ministry: not that during the course of his life he ought to cease being of service to society, or that, endowed with such integrity of mind and such talent of eloquence, he can continue too long in the exercise of so noble an employment; but because it is fitting that he should guard against degrading his character, by doing anything which may fall short of what he has already done. The orator is indebted for what he is, not only to knowledge, which increases with his years, but to his voice, lungs, and strength of body; and when the latter are impaired by years, or debilitated by infirmities, it is to be feared that something might be lacking in this great man, either from his stopping short through fatigue, and out of breath at every effort, or by not making himself sufficiently heard, or, lastly, by expecting, and not finding, him to be what he formerly was.

When the orator does sound a retreat, no less ample fruits of study will attend on him. He either will write the history of his time for the instruction of posterity, or he will explain the law to those who came to ask his advice, or he will write a treatise on eloquence, or that worthy mouth of his will employ itself in inculcating the finest moral precepts. As was customary with the ancients, well-disposed youth will frequent his house, consulting him as an oracle on the true manner of speaking. As the parent of eloquence will he form them, and as an old experienced pilot will he give them an account of shores, and harbors, and what are the presages of storms, and what may be required for working the ship in contrary or favorable winds. To all this will he be induced not only by a duty of humanity common to mankind, but also by a certain pleasure in it; for no one would be glad to see an art going into decay, in which he himself excelled, and what is more laudable than to teach others that in which one is perfectly skilled?

For all I know, the happiest time in an orator's life is when he has retired from the world to devote himself to rest; and, remote from envy, and remote from strife, he looks back on his reputation, as from a harbor of safety; and while still living has a sense of that veneration which commonly awaits only the dead; thus anticipating the pleasure of the noble impression posterity will conceive of him. I am conscious that to the extent of my poor ability, whatever I knew before, and whatever I could collect for the service of this work, I have candidly and ingenuously made a communication of, for the instruction of those who might be willing to reap any advantage from it: and it is enough for an honest man to have taught what he knows.

To be good men, which is the first and most important thing, consists chiefly in the will, and whoever has a sincere desire to be a man of integrity, will easily learn the arts that teach virtue; and these arts are not involved in so many perplexities, neither are they of such great number, as not to be learned by a few years' application. The ordering of an upright and happy life is attainable by an easy and compendious method, when inclination is not lacking. Nature begot us with the best dispositions, and it is so easy to the well-inclined to learn that which is good, that we can not help being surprized, on making a due estimate of things, how there can be so many bad persons in the world. For, as water is naturally a proper element for fish, dry land for quadrupeds, and air for birds, so indeed it ought to be more easy to live according to the prescript of nature than to infringe her laws.

As to the rest, tho we might measure our age, not by the space of more advanced years, but by the time of youth, we should find that we had quite years enough for learning, all things being made shorter by order, method, and the manner of application. To bring the matter home to our oratorical studies, of what significance is the custom which I see kept up by many, of declaiming so many years in schools, and of expending so much labor on imaginary subjects, when in a moderate time the rules of eloquence may be learned, and pursuant to their directions, a real image framed of the contests at the bar? By this I do not mean to hint in the least that exercises for speaking should ever be discontinued, but rather that none should grow old in any one particular exercise for that purpose, for we may require the knowledge of many sciences, and learn the precepts of morality, and exercise ourselves in such causes as are agitated at the bar, even while we continue in the state of scholars. And indeed the art of oratory is such as need not require many years for learning it. Each of the arts I have mentioned may be abridged into few books, there being no occasion to consider them so minutely and so much in detail. Practise remains, which soon makes us well skilled in them. Knowledge of things is increasing daily, and yet books are not so many; it is necessary to read in order to acquire this knowledge, of which either examples as to the things themselves may be met with in history, or the eloquent expression of them may be found in orators. It is also necessary that we should read the opinions of philosophers and lawyers, with some other things deserving of notice.

TAKING TIME FOR STUDY

All this indeed may be compassed, but we ourselves are the cause of our not having time enough. How small a portion of it do we allot to our studies! A good part of it is spent in frivolous compliments and paying and returning visits, a good part of it is taken up in the telling of idle stories, a good part at the public spectacles, and a good part in the pleasures of the table. Add to these our great variety of amusements, and that extravagant indulgence we bestow upon our bodies. One time we must go on a course of travels, another time we wish recreation amidst the pleasures of rural life, and another time we are full of painful solicitude regarding the state of our fortune, calculating and balancing our loss and gain; and together with these, how often do we give ourselves up to the intoxication of wine, and in what a multiplicity of voluptuousness does our profligate mind suffer itself to be immersed? Should there be an interval for study amidst these avocations, can it be said to be proper? But were we to devote all this idle or ill-spent time to study, should we not find life long enough and time more than enough for becoming learned? This is evident by only computing the time of the day, besides the advantages of the night, of which a good part is more than sufficient for sleep. But we now preposterously compute not the years we have studied, but the years we have lived. Tho geometricians and grammarians, and the professors of other arts, spent all their lives, however long, in treating and discussing their respective arts, does it thence follow that we must have as many lives as there are things to be learned? But they did not extend the learning of them to old age, being content with learning them only, and they spent so many years not so much in their study as in their practise.

Now, tho one should despair of reaching to the height of perfection, a groundless hope even in a person of genius, health, talent, and with masters to assist him; yet it is noble, as Cicero says, to have a place in the second, or third, rank. He who can not rival the glory of Achilles in military exploits, shall not therefore have a mean opinion of the praise due to Ajax, or Diomedes, and he who can not approach Homer, need not despise the fame of Tyrteus. If men were to yield to the thought of imagining none capable of exceeding such eminent persons as went before them, then they even who are deemed excellent would not have been so. Vergil would not have excelled Lucretius and Macer; nor Cicero, Crassus and Hortensius; and no one for the future would pretend to any advantage over his predecessor.

Tho the hope of surpassing these great men be but faint, yet it is an honor to follow them. Have Pollio and Messala, who began to appear at the bar when Cicero was already possest of the empire of eloquence, acquired little dignity in their life-time, and left but a small degree of glory for the remembrance of posterity? True it is that arts brought to perfection would deserve very ill of human affairs if afterward they could not at least be kept to the same standard.

THE REWARDS OF ELOQUENCE

Add to this that a moderate share of eloquence is attended with no small advantage, and if measured by the fruits gathered from it, will almost be on a par with that which is perfect. It would be no difficult matter to show from many ancient or modern examples that no other profession acquires for men, greater honors, wealth, friendship, present and future glory, were it not degrading to the honor of letters to divert the mind from the contemplation of the most noble object, the study and possession of which is such a source of contentment, and fix it on the less momentous rewards it may have, not unlike those who say they do not so much seek virtue as the pleasure resulting from it.

Let us therefore with all the zealous impulses of our heart endeavor to attain the very majesty of eloquence, than which the immortal gods have not imparted anything better to mankind, and without which all would be mute in nature, and destitute of the splendor of a perfect glory and future remembrance. Let us likewise always make continued progress toward perfection, and by so doing we shall either reach the height, or at least shall see many beneath us.

This is all, as far as in me lies, I could contribute to the promoting and perfecting of the art of eloquence; the knowledge of which, if it does not prove of any great advantage to studious youth, will, at least, what I more heartily wish for, give them a more ardent desire for doing well.

www.ingramcontent.com/pod-product-compliance
Lightning Source LLC
Chambersburg PA
CBHW081122080526
44587CB00021B/3717